SUPER SIMPLE
WETLAND
CRITTER CRAFTS

Fun and Easy Animal Crafts

Sammy Bosch

Consulting Editor, Diane Craig, M.A./Reading Specialist

Super Sandcastle

An Imprint of Abdo Publishing
abdopublishing.com

abdopublishing.com

Published by Abdo Publishing, a division of ABDO, PO Box 398166, Minneapolis, Minnesota 55439. Copyright © 2017 by Abdo Consulting Group, Inc. International copyrights reserved in all countries. No part of this book may be reproduced in any form without written permission from the publisher. Super SandCastle™ is a trademark and logo of Abdo Publishing.

Printed in the United States of America, North Mankato, Minnesota
062016
092016

Editor: Liz Salzmann
Content Developer: Nancy Tuminelly
Craft Production: Frankie Tuminelly
Cover and Interior Design and Production: Colleen Dolphin, Mighty Media, Inc.
Photo Credits: Mighty Media, Inc.; Shutterstock
The following manufacturers/names appearing in this book are trademarks:
Elmer's® Glue-All®, Scribbles®, Sharpie®

Library of Congress Cataloging-in-Publication Data
Names: Bosch, Sammy, author.
Title: Super simple wetland critter crafts : fun and easy animal crafts / by Sammy Bosch ; consulting editor, Diane Craig, M.A./reading specialist.
Other titles: Wetland critter crafts
Description: Minneapolis, Minnesota : Abdo Publishing, [2017] | Series: Super simple critter crafts
Identifiers: LCCN 2016001382 (print) | LCCN 2016008554 (ebook) | ISBN 9781680781649 (print) | ISBN 9781680776072 (ebook)
Subjects: LCSH: Handicraft--Juvenile literature. | Wetland animals--Juvenile literature.
Classification: LCC TT160 .B7578 2017 (print) | LCC TT160 (ebook) | DDC 745.59--dc23
LC record available at http://lccn.loc.gov/2016001382

Super SandCastle™ books are created by a team of professional educators, reading specialists, and content developers around five essential components—phonemic awareness, phonics, vocabulary, text comprehension, and fluency—to assist young readers as they develop reading skills and strategies and increase their general knowledge. All books are written, reviewed, and leveled for guided reading and early reading intervention programs for use in shared, guided, and independent reading and writing activities to support a balanced approach to literacy instruction.

TO ADULT HELPERS

The craft projects in this series are fun and simple. There are just a few things to remember to keep kids safe. Some projects require the use of sharp or hot objects. Also, kids may be using messy materials such as glue or paint. Make sure they protect their clothes and work surfaces. Review the projects before starting, and be ready to assist when necessary.

. . . .

KEY SYMBOL

Watch for this warning symbol in this book. Here is what it means.

 HOT!
You will be working with something hot. Get help from an adult!

CONTENTS

WETLAND CRITTERS

A wetland is an area of land that is wet or partly filled with water. There are many different critters living in wetlands! They live in the water and mud.

You can make your own wetland critters for your home! Make some fun crafts and learn more about wetland animals.

GET TO KNOW WETLAND ANIMALS!

FUN FACTS ABOUT YOUR FAVORITE WETLAND ANIMALS

DUCKS

The mallard is the most common type of duck. The males have green feathers on their heads.

TURTLES

Turtles have existed for more than 200 million years.

FROGS

Most frogs need water to survive. They **absorb** oxygen from water through their skin.

aLLIGaTORS

The American alligator can bite harder than almost any other animal. Wild alligators live up to 50 years.

OTTERS

Otters can stay underwater for up to 8 minutes. Their ears and **nostrils** close to keep the water out.

FISH

There are nearly 28,000 kinds of fish in the world!

MUSKRATS

Muskrats make a smelly liquid called "musk." They use it to warn other animals away and mark their territories.

saLaMaNDERS

If a predator grabs a salamander's tail, the tail breaks off. The salamander escapes and grows a new tail!

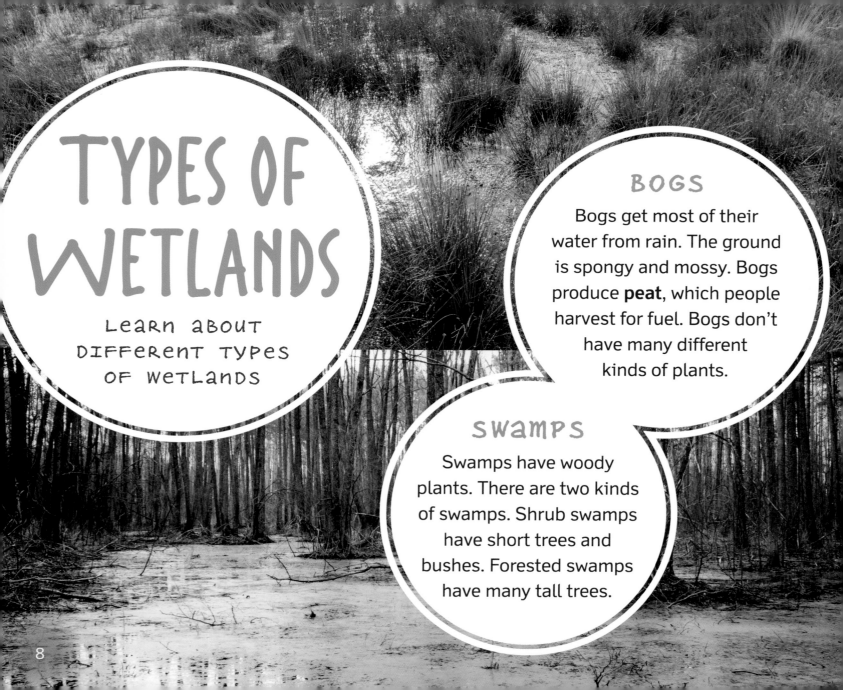

TYPES OF WETLANDS

LEARN ABOUT DIFFERENT TYPES OF WETLANDS

BOGS

Bogs get most of their water from rain. The ground is spongy and mossy. Bogs produce **peat**, which people harvest for fuel. Bogs don't have many different kinds of plants.

SWAMPS

Swamps have woody plants. There are two kinds of swamps. Shrub swamps have short trees and bushes. Forested swamps have many tall trees.

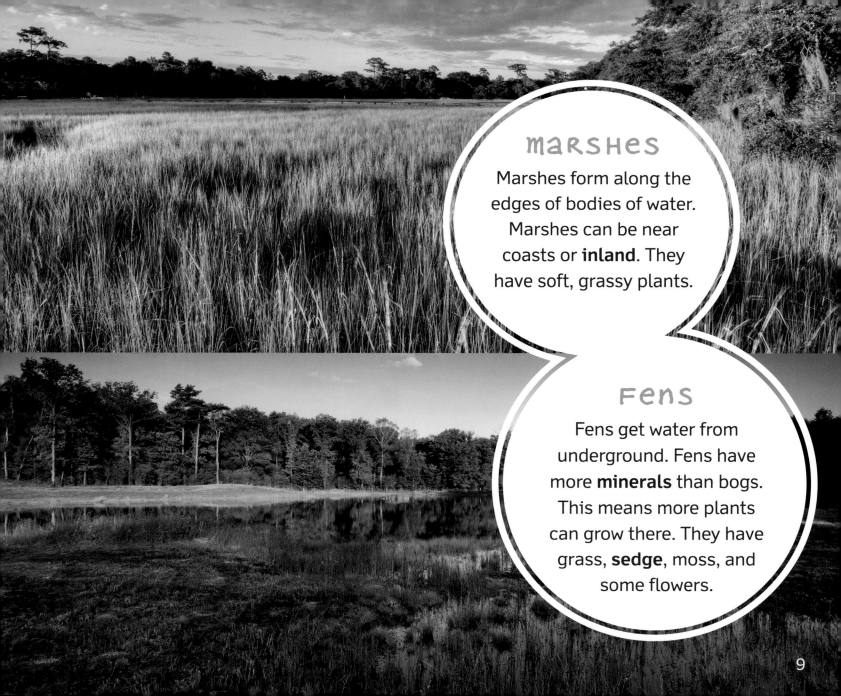

marshes

Marshes form along the edges of bodies of water. Marshes can be near coasts or **inland**. They have soft, grassy plants.

Fens

Fens get water from underground. Fens have more **minerals** than bogs. This means more plants can grow there. They have grass, **sedge**, moss, and some flowers.

9

MATERIALS

Here are some of the things you'll need to do the projects.

acrylic paint

brown yarn

CDs

chenille stems

craft feathers

craft foam

craft glue

egg carton

felt

foam cups

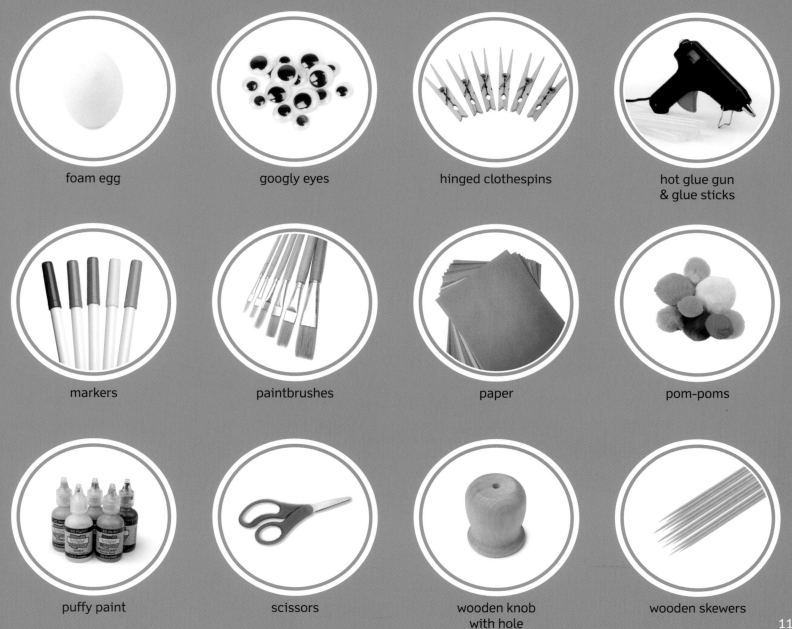

foam egg

googly eyes

hinged clothespins

hot glue gun
& glue sticks

markers

paintbrushes

paper

pom-poms

puffy paint

scissors

wooden knob
with hole

wooden skewers

11

EGG-CELLENT TURTLE

THIS LITTLE CUTIE WON'T CRAWL AWAY!

MATERIALS

egg carton	paintbrush	craft glue
scissors	green craft foam	2 googly eyes
newspaper	ruler	green pom-pom
green acrylic paint		

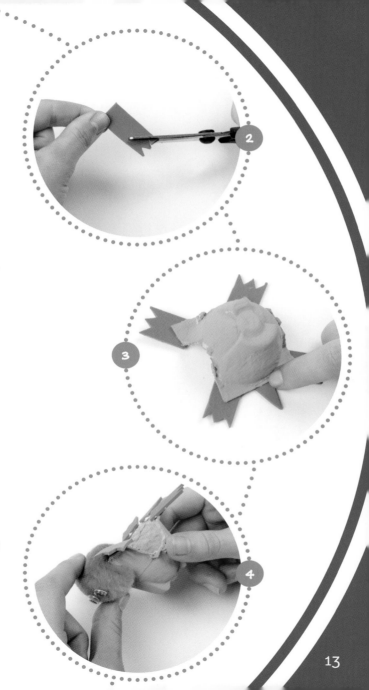

1. Cut one cup off of the egg carton. Cover your work surface with newspaper. Paint the outside of the cup green. Let the paint dry.

2. Cut four rectangles out of green craft foam. Make each piece 1 by ¾ inches (2.5 by 2 cm). These are the legs. Cut two triangles out of one end of each leg to make feet. Glue the straight end of each leg to a corner of the egg cup.

3. Cut a thin triangle out of green foam for the tail. Glue it to the egg cup.

4. Glue the googly eyes to the pom-pom. Put glue on the pom-pom above the eyes. Slide the glued area over the edge of the egg carton. Let the glue dry.

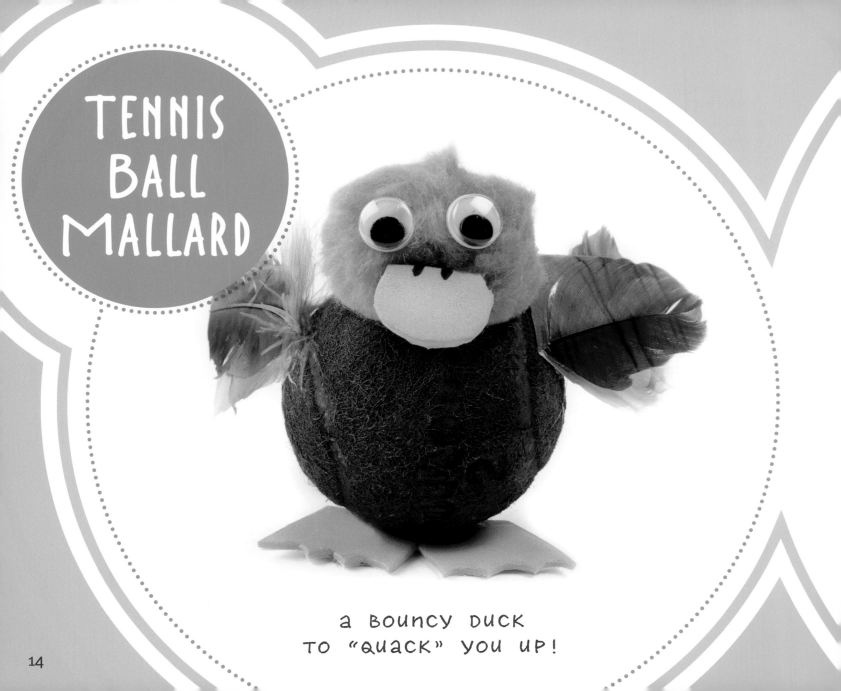

TENNIS BALL MALLARD

A BOUNCY DUCK
TO "QUACK" YOU UP!

MATERIALS

newspaper	orange craft foam	large green pom-pom
tennis ball	ruler	craft glue
brown acrylic paint	scissors	2 googly eyes
paintbrush	black marker	brown craft feathers

1 Cover your work surface with newspaper. Paint the tennis ball brown. Let it dry.

2 Cut two 1-inch (2.5 cm) circles out of orange craft foam. Cut the side of each circle so it has a straight edge. These will be the duck's bill. Draw two black marks on one circle for **nostrils**.

3 Glue the straight edge of each piece of orange foam to the pom-pom. Put the one with the nostrils on top.

4 Glue the googly eyes above the bill. Glue the pom-pom to the tennis ball.

5 Draw duck feet on orange craft foam. Cut them out. Glue them to the tennis ball.

6 Glue brown feathers to each side of the tennis ball. Let the glue dry.

SPRINGY BOBBLE FROG

an egg-carton frog that bobbles and wobbles!

MATERIALS

egg carton
scissors
newspaper
wooden knob with hole

acrylic paint,
  various colors
paintbrush
craft glue
ruler

2 chenille stems
2 pom-poms
2 googly eyes
pencil

1. Cut three cups off of the egg carton. Cut two of them in half **horizontally** to make the cups more shallow. **Discard** the parts you cut off.

2. Cover your work surface with newspaper. Paint the wooden knob and the egg cups. Let the paint dry. Add colored spots to the egg cups. Let the paint dry.

3. Glue the bottom of a small cup to the bottom of the large cup.

4. Cut a 3-inch (8 cm) piece of pink chenille stem. Curl one end. Bend the other end.

(continued on next page)

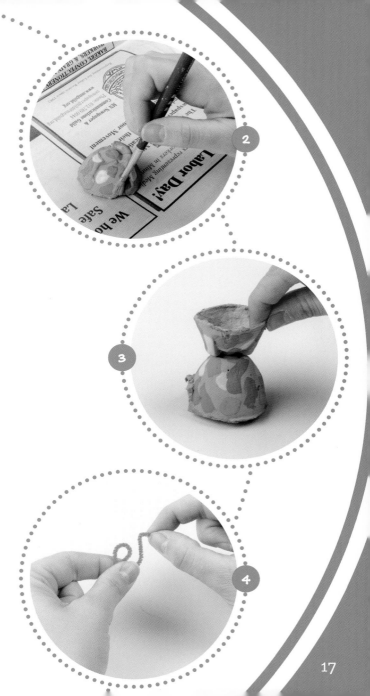

17

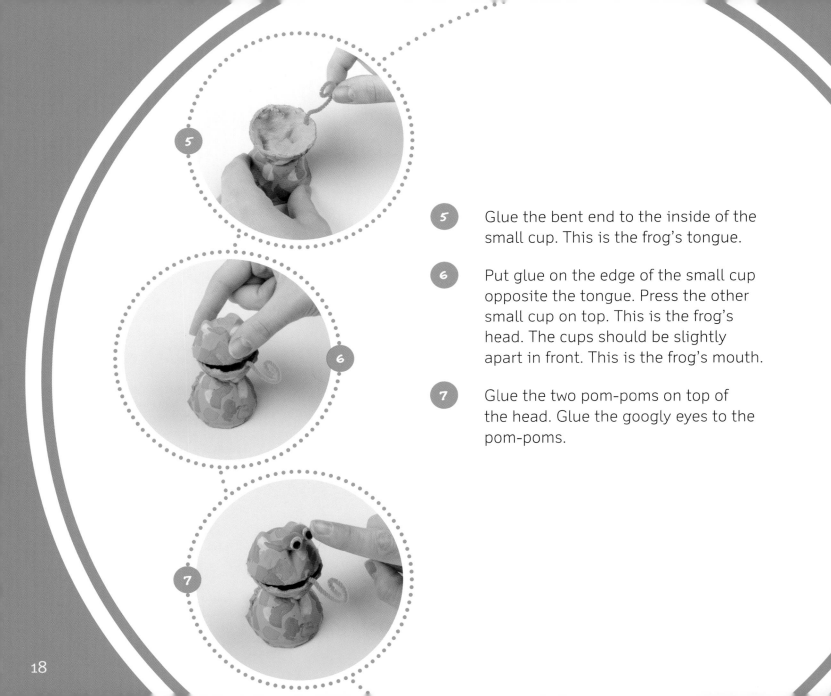

5 Glue the bent end to the inside of the small cup. This is the frog's tongue.

6 Put glue on the edge of the small cup opposite the tongue. Press the other small cup on top. This is the frog's head. The cups should be slightly apart in front. This is the frog's mouth.

7 Glue the two pom-poms on top of the head. Glue the googly eyes to the pom-poms.

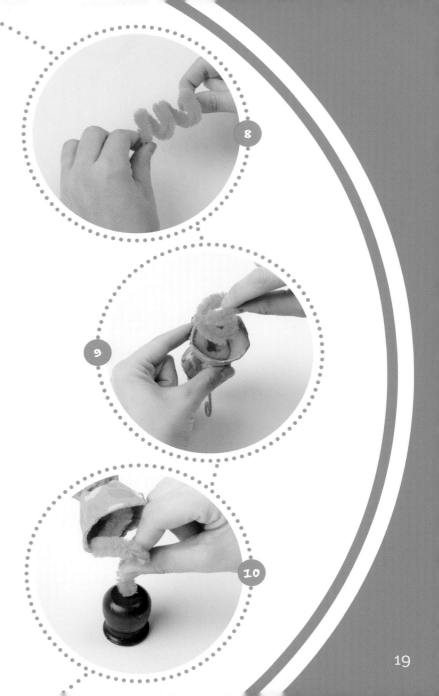

8. Cut an 8-inch (20 cm) piece of the other chenille stem. Wrap it around a pencil. Slide it off the pencil. This makes a spring.

9. Glue one end of the spring inside the bottom of the frog's body. Let the glue dry.

10. Stick the other end of the spring into the small hole in the knob.

11. Press the frog gently over the knob. Let go. Watch the frog wobble!

19

SCALY SHIMMERING FISH

TURN CDS INTO a SHINY FISH!

MATERIALS

2 CDs	craft glue	scissors
permanent marker	colored paper	string
decorations such as gems & sequins	pencil	

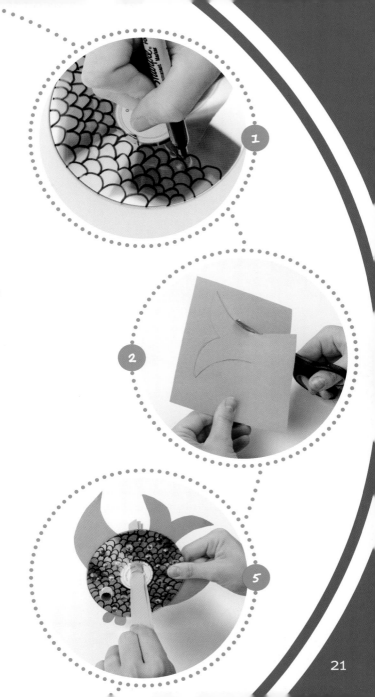

1. Draw scales on the shiny side of each CD with the permanent marker. Glue decorations on each CD. Be creative!

2. Draw fins for the top and bottom of the fish on colored paper. Cut them out. Draw a mouth and tail on colored paper. Cut them out.

3. Glue the paper features to the undecorated side of one CD. Make sure they stick out. Glue the other CD on top. Glue a googly eye on each side of the fish. Let the glue dry.

4. Fold the long edge of a sheet of paper ½ inch (1.3 cm). Turn the paper over. Fold the edge ½ inch (1.3 cm) again. Repeat flipping and folding until the paper is folded into a fan.

5. Stick the folded paper through the hole in the CDs. Gently spread the folds apart on each side. This makes the side fins.

6. Push a piece of string through the hole in the fish. Tie the ends together. Hang up your fish!

21

CRAWLING CUP ALLIGATOR

THIS GREEN GATOR
IS SUPER COOL!

newspaper
2 foam cups
green acrylic paint
paintbrush

hot glue gun
   & glue sticks
white paper
ruler
scissors

black craft foam
2 large white pom-
   poms
4 green chenille stems

1. Cover your work surface with newspaper. Paint the cups green. Let the paint dry.

2. Glue the tops of the cups together. This is the alligator's body.

3. Cut a strip out of white paper. Make it 1 by 7 inches (3 by 18 cm). Cut triangles out of one long side to make teeth. Glue the teeth around one end of the body.

4. Cut two circles out of black craft foam. Glue one to each white pom-pom. These are the eyes. Glue them to the top of the body in the middle.

5. Bend a *W* shape in the middle of a chenille stem. This is a foot. Twist the rest of the stem together to make a leg. Repeat with the other chenille stems.

6. Glue the legs to the body. Bend the feet out. Let the glue dry.

HUNGRY RIVER OTTER

an OTTER
TO DECORATE
YOUR ROOM!

MATERIALS

2 small paper plates
scissors
ruler
craft glue

black, brown & blue felt
2 googly eyes
large paper plate

newspaper
gray acrylic paint
paintbrush

1. Cut one of the small paper plates in half. Fold in both sides of one half. This creates a triangle with a flat top.

2. Cut a curve in the middle of the round edge of the triangle.

3. Cut each side off about ½ inch (1.3 cm) from the folds. There should be a flap on each side.

(continued on next page)

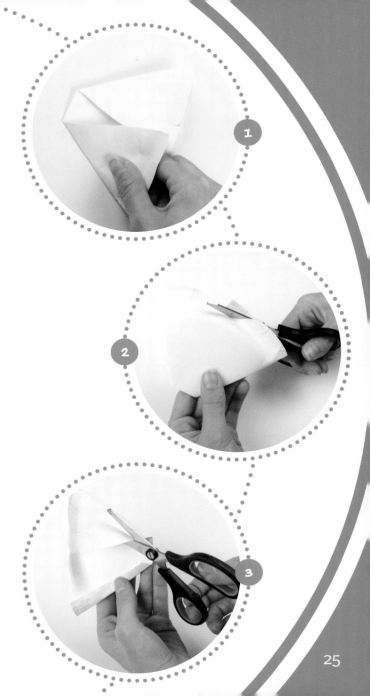

25

4. Put glue on the flaps on the triangle. Press the triangle onto the other small plate. This is the otter's **snout**.

5. Cut a small circle out of black felt for the nose. Glue it to the snout. Glue the googly eyes to the plate above the snout. That completes the otter's head.

6. Lay the large paper plate upside down. This is the otter's body. Glue the head to it. **Overlap** the plates.

7. Cover your work surface with newspaper. Paint the edge of the body gray. Paint the top and bottom of the head. Paint the top of the snout.

8. Cut a long, thin triangle out of brown felt. This is the tail. Turn the otter over. Glue the tail to the bottom of the body.

9. Cut two rectangles out of brown felt. Make them about 3 inches (7.5 cm) long. These are the legs. Cut three round toes on one end of each rectangle. Glue the legs on either side of the tail.

10. Cut two more rectangles out of brown felt for the arms. Make them about 5 inches (13 cm) long. Round off one end of each arm to make a paw. Glue the straight ends of the arms to the back of the body.

11. Cut two 1½-inch (4 cm) circles out of brown felt. These are the ears. Glue them to the back of the head.

12. Cut a fish out of blue felt. Turn the otter over. Glue the fish to one of the otter's paws. Glue both paws to the front of the body.

FUZZY MUSKRAT

a "MUSK-DO" FOR
animaL LOVERS!

28

MATERIALS

3-inch (7.5 cm) foam egg

plastic knife

newspaper

brown acrylic paint

paintbrush

brown yarn

scissors

ruler

wooden skewer

light brown felt

craft glue

2 googly eyes

small black bead

puffy paint

1. Cut a **slice** from the long side of the egg so it will sit flat. Cover your work surface with newspaper. Paint one end of the egg brown. This will be the muskrat's face.

2. Cut about 80 pieces of yarn. Make each piece 3 inches (8 cm) long. Fold a yarn piece in half. Push the fold into the egg with the skewer. Keep adding yarn until every part of the muskrat except the face is covered.

3. Cut two ovals out of light brown felt. Push one end of each oval into the egg near the edge of the yarn. These are the muskrat's ears.

4. Glue the googly eyes onto the face. Glue the bead on for the nose. Draw a mouth with puffy paint.

5. Cut three 10-inch (25 cm) pieces of brown yarn. Tie them together at one end. Braid the yarn. Tie the end in a knot. This is the muskrat's tail. Glue the tail to the back of the muskrat.

COLORFUL STRIPED SALAMANDER

CLIP THIS BRIGHT
SALAMANDER ON ALL
KINDS OF STUFF!

MATERIALS

hinged clothespin	craft glue	pencil
markers	red chenille stem	2 small pom-poms
white & green paper	ruler	2 googly eyes
scissors		

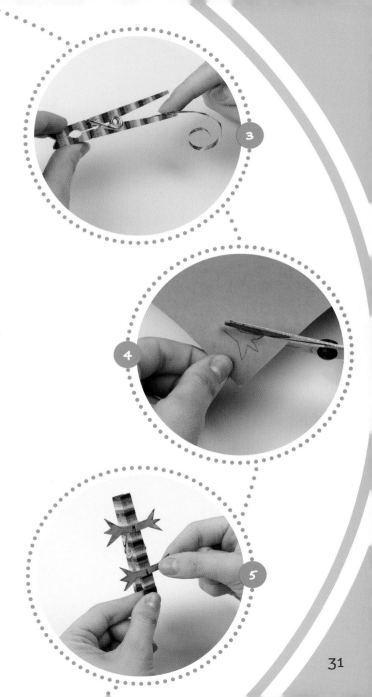

1. Use markers to color stripes on the clothespin.

2. Cut a long, thin triangle out of white paper. Make one side as wide as the clothespin. This is the tail. Color stripes on both sides of the tail. Roll the paper to curl the end of the tail.

3. Glue the uncurled end of the tail to the back of the clothespin.

4. Draw feet on green paper. Cut them out.

5. Glue the feet to the bottom of the clothespin. Color the toes red.

6. Cut a 1½-inch (4 cm) piece of red chenille stem. Wrap it around a pencil. Remove the pencil. Glue one end of the stem in the front of the clothespin. This is the salamander's tongue.

7. Glue a googly eye to each pom-pom. Glue the pom-poms to the top of the clothespin.

GLOSSARY

absorb – to soak up or take in.

discard – to throw away.

horizontally – in the same direction as the ground, or side to side.

inland – on land that is not near the coast.

mineral – a chemical element that occurs naturally in the ground.

nostril – an opening in the nose.

overlap – to make something lie partly on top of something else.

peat – partly rotten plants found in wet areas such as bogs and swamps.

sedge – a type of grasslike plant that grows in wetlands.

slice – a piece cut from something such as a pizza or cake.

snout – the jaws and nose of an animal.

JACK NICKLAUS
MY MOST MEMORABLE SHOTS IN THE MAJORS

JACK NICKLAUS
MY MOST MEMORABLE SHOTS IN THE MAJORS

By Jack Nicklaus with Ken Bowden

Foreword by Barbara Nicklaus
Illustrations by Jim McQueen

A GOLF DIGEST BOOK

Published by Golf Digest/Tennis, Inc.
A New York Times Company
5520 Park Avenue, Box 395
Trumbull, CT 06611-0395

Manufactured in the
United States of America

Illustrations by Jim McQueen
Book design by Nick DiDio

Library of Congress Cataloging-in-Publication Data

Nicklaus, Jack.
   My most memorable shots in the majors.

   "A Golf Digest book."
   1. Golf. 2. Golf—Tournaments. I. Bowden, Ken.
II. Title.
GV965.N514 1988   796.352'7   87-37352
ISBN 0-8129-1750-2

**TO
KEN BOWDEN**

who made most of
the journey, too,
with thanks for
his friendship,
his patience, and
his enthusiasm for
telling it right.

CONTENTS

FOREWORD
by
Barbara Nicklaus

TO BE SUCCESSFUL,
YOU CAN NOT BE AFRAID TO FAIL

Golf's major championships have always been important in our lives. When Jack and I met the first week of our freshman year at Ohio State University, Jack had just returned from participating in the United States Amateur Championship. I knew nothing about golf at the time, but I was immediately aware of how important this tournament was to him and how disappointed he had been with his performance.

Two years later, in 1959, he was to win the first of his two U.S. Amateur Championships, and by then I was beginning to understand his mental as well as physical approach to the game. I had never met anyone as determined or as dedicated, and I somehow knew that he would be successful in whatever he chose to do in life. He had had some tough matches at the Broadmoor Golf Club that week, but he had thought and played his way through them perfectly.

We became engaged that year on Christmas Eve, and were married the following July (the weekend of the PGA Championship, I might add, because that was the only tournament Jack definitely could not play in as an amateur!).

I am really proud to say that Jack and I have shared the happiness of *all* of his 20 "major" victories. I have only missed being with him (in person) for three of them—the 1959 and 1961 U.S. Amateurs and the 1963 Masters. To me, one of the great things about Jack is that he has always accepted and treated golf as a game that he truly enjoys playing for its own sake. He is most fortunate to be completely happy in his chosen career.

Major tournament wins *and* other tournament victories seemed to come fast and easy to Jack during his first five years as a professional golfer (1962-1967). Then, suddenly, 1968 and 1969 saw no "major" victories. His father, whom he adored, became ill with cancer in the fall of 1969, and we lost him in February of 1970. You might say that this was the first major tragedy in Jack's life, and he felt as though he had let his dad down in the last years of his life. Victories had come so easily, and he real-

ized that he had been relying on his talent and had stopped working as hard as he should have been. As we have all said at one time or another, some good comes out of all bad, and his dad's death renewed Jack's interest and determination and gave him the incentive to live up to his potential and to put everything he had into the game. He won the British Open Championship at St. Andrews in Scotland that year, and, although we never discussed it, I'm sure we both thought of that special victory as a tribute to his dad.

Of course, along with the victories, we have shared many more defeats. It's easy to be a winner, but Jack has always been most gracious in defeat. To be successful, you can not be afraid to fail.

No defeat is easy, but when I think of "defeat" there are probably two tournaments that come to mind immediately—the 1971 Masters and the 1983 United States Open Championship. Jack had birdied the first hole in the last round of the '71 Masters, and felt that he was confidently on his way to a fourth victory. At the end of the day, Charles Coody was crowned the Masters champion, and I took a dejected Jack home with me that night. We went to the Bahamas the following week with the children for a few days of fishing and relaxation, and he decided that he would not even play in the Tournament of Champions the next week. He was *really* down on himself. This was not like Jack, and—for the first time—I decided to interfere! I told him that he would look like a "spoiled child" if he did not play. I made our airline reservations and said, *"We are going!"* (another first for me). This episode fortunately had a happy ending, as he won the Tournament of Champions that year by eight strokes. I breathed a sigh of relief, Jack was happy with himself, and he once again showed his determination to be the best.

The 1982 United States Open Championship defeat probably hit Jack the hardest of all. He was 42 years old, the victories were not as abundant, and he had completed 72 holes of play thinking that he had "probably" just won his fifth U.S. Open. Jack watched on a TV monitor as Tom Watson hit into the rough at the par-3 17th hole, and, knowing what a tough shot Tom had ahead of him, he felt even more secure. As all golf historians know, Tom hit probably the most spectacular shot of his career, holing out for a birdie and going on to win his first United States Open Championship. It took Jack a long time to recover from that defeat, but those kinds of shots always make golf the real winner.

Other defeats were glaring and naturally uncomfortable, but perhaps Jack's greatest strength is his ability to accept defeat and move on with more determination than ever.

I am so flattered that Jack asked me to write the foreword for this book. It somehow seemed right, since we have shared the results of every shot in the book—either with quiet and/or quick eye contact, a pat, a hug, a phone call, or arm in arm. I guess you can tell that I love and admire this man deeply, and that his most memorable shots are also "mine."

I hope you will enjoy reliving Jack's Most Memorable Shots in the Majors with him.

HOW TO
USE THIS BOOK

I go into every tournament determined to give each shot 100 percent effort, right from the opening drive. That's because the reality of stroke play, which is the name of the pro game, is that every shot counts equally.

I also come out of most tournaments, and especially the major championships, with just one or two strokes seared into my memory. That's because logic is no match for human nature. The shots remain memorable to me because—although in reality they were no more important than any of the others—at the time they seemed especially critical or dramatic. Mostly, they are shots that occurred in the final round, and generally on the back nine when the pressure was peak.

These are the shots—good and bad—I'll be telling you about in this new book.

I think there are a couple of general lessons to be learned from the shots that stick in any golfer's mind, whether his goal is winning the Grand Slam or simply the last flight of the club championship.

The way to benefit from your good shots is simply to bring them to the front of your consciousness whenever you're in a comparable playing situation. Tell yourself: "I've executed this successfully before, so there's no reason I can't do it again." If you have my kind of vivid recall, that can be a huge help both technically and in combating pressure.

Making use of the bad shots is harder because instinctively you want to shove them out of your mind. I won't let myself do that until I believe I've mastered and memorized the antidote, whether that involves hours on the practice tee, or, as is more usual, disciplining myself to better observe, analyze and visualize —that is, think—on the course itself. The longer I've played golf, the clearer it's become that the learning process is endless, so in recent years particularly I've used my bad shots as the spur to continue my schooling. If you really care about winning, I think you'll find this a rewarding habit.

And that's how this book can help you. If you study what I learned in the heat of battle you can become just as good a student. You'll learn how to think a round of golf through. You'll learn from your mistakes and you'll learn from your winners—and when to repeat them.

Jack Nicklaus

**The 1959
U.S. Amateur**
Broadmoor Golf Club,
Colorado Springs, Colo.

17th hole, par 5, 613 yards

THE SITUATION: One up against Gene Andrews starting the 35th hole of our semifinal match, a 613-yard par 5, I can't resist trying the impossible: to drive the green from the tee. Result: a bad hook, followed by three more hacks, leaving me with a 25-foot putt to match Gene's effortless par and keep what almost certainly will be a critical edge going to the final hole.

MY THOUGHT PROCESS: For the first 18 feet the ball will travel along the almost flat upper tier of the green, but then will dive sharply to the lower plateau at about a 15-degree angle. Looking the putt over carefully from all perspectives, I remember that in the previous rounds there has been something a little different about this green: For some reason the grass is heavier, so it's played slower than the others all week. That reminds me to stroke the ball firmer, which should help on two accounts. First, I needn't fight my gushing adrenaline. Second, I can go at the putt do-or-die, because if I miss the hole it's history anyway.

THE SHOT: With any sharply breaking putt, and particularly downhill, you must first very carefully identify your *starting* line, then commit to it totally at address with blade and body alignment. If you don't, you'll try to reroute the putt with your stroke, which is death. Next, you'll retain smoothness and good tempo by swinging longer rather than hitting harder—by not trying to *force* the distance, especially when your nerves are jumping. Third, you'll improve your chances by rehearsing the longer stroke deliberately a number of times, and calm those butterflies by taking some deep breaths while you do so. I manage all those things on this monster. I can the putt to halve the hole, close Gene out on the next and am in my first national championship final.

THE LESSON: Be observant in previous rounds, *remember* what you experience and go for broke when it can cost you no more dearly if you fail.

GOT TO MAKE IT

**The 1959
U.S. Amateur
Championship**
Broadmoor Golf Club
Colorado Springs, Colo.
18th hole, par 4, 430 yards

PLAYER'S SHOT

THE SITUATION: It is the 36th hole of the final match and I'm all square with Charles Coe after making him a gift of the previous hole following a terrible drive. Charles hit a lovely 3-wood to Position A, and I've followed with an equally good one that has stopped six feet ahead of his ball. Charles hits a great-looking 8-iron dead at the flag, but it doesn't bite enough on the hard green and finishes over the back, leaving him with a tricky little pitch.

MY THOUGHT PROCESS: I've already decided the shot is an 8-iron for me, too, and actually have the club in my hand. But the way Charles' ball bounced and ran produces second thoughts. Finally, I decide to play a semi-punch shot with a 9-iron, aiming to fly the ball in low, landing it on the front of the green and hoping it will run back to the hole. I figure that, even if the ball doesn't run far enough, at least I'll be putting, which is always a higher percentage shot than a chip or pitch.

THE SHOT: I position the ball back just inside my right heel instead of opposite my left instep, but keep my hands in their normal position opposite the left thigh, thereby reducing the club's effective loft. Then I toe-in the clubface very slightly, both to keep the ball down and make it run more by imparting a little right-to-left sidespin. I make a normal swing, but a firm one, and with a special effort not to roll my hands through impact, so that the clubface will not close too quickly. The ball behaves exactly as I've planned, landing on the front of the green and running up eight feet short of the cup. Charles plays a beautifully delicate little pitch that almost falls into the hole, but when I make the eight-footer, I've won my first national title.

THE LESSON: Whenever you can watch an opponent hit first, in match play or stroke play, do so and *learn.* Try to figure the club being used, and study the ball's flight and its behavior on landing extra carefully. Then apply what you've observed to your own strategy.

EVEN IF IT'S HOGAN, DON'T BE

THE SITUATION: Walking after my 3-wood tee shot on the 385-yard 13th hole in the final round, a scoreboard indicates that I'm leading the championship by one stroke ahead of Arnold Palmer, Julius Boros and Jack Fleck. I've put the ball exactly where I want it, on level ground short of the creek intersecting the fairway, and loft an easy 9-iron 12 feet below the pin. My playing partner, for the first time ever, is Ben Hogan, going for a record fifth Open and now two shots adrift of me.

MY THOUGHT PROCESS: At only 20 years old, I'm still in awe of Hogan, although he's been very pleasant to me. Nevertheless, as I look over the birdie putt, it occurs to me that even he might have difficulty in making up three strokes in five holes. Pumped by that notion, I stroke the ball a little too hard and it slides 18 inches past the cup. Now there's a little indentation left by a poorly repaired ball mark between me and the hole.

THE SHOT: Excited, anxious, under as much pressure as I've ever known, I can't focus my mind clearly on whether the rules allow me to repair the ball mark (they do). Also, I'm too shy or embarrassed to admit this in front of Hogan or to hold up play by asking an official. So I go ahead and stroke the putt. The mark deflects the ball just enough to spin it out. I bogey, then three-putt the next green. Arnie, with his phenomenal historic charge, wins the Open with me second.

INTIMIDATED

**The 1960
U. S. Open
Championship**
Cherry Hills Country Club,
Denver, Colo.
13th hole, par 4, 385 yards

THE LESSON: There are three lessons here, which have stuck with me ever since. First: Repair ball marks as you'd like others to repair them for you. Second: Know the rules. Third: If in doubt, ask.

The 1961 U.S. Open
Oakland Hills Country Club
Birmingham, Mich.
18th hole, par 4,
459 yards

KNOW WHEN NOT TO GAMBLE

THE SITUATION: I'm still an amateur, but I'm hot to make amends for finishing second in the Open to Arnold Palmer the year before. I arrive a week early, am inspired by a couple of practice rounds with Ben Hogan, and, trying to lose a little weight, play 36 holes a day. Warming up before the first round I feel "ready." Walking up the 18th hole four hours later I feel about ready to slit my throat. I'm four over par and have missed the green yet again—and in an awful place.

MY THOUGHT PROCESS: My ball is in rough down behind a wide and deep trap fronted by a sharply rising mound. The pin is just beyond the mound. To get the ball close would require extreme delicacy, plus a big serving of luck. The temptation to try the shot is almost irresistible. I just cannot afford to drop any more strokes. On the other hand, if I miss this one I'm looking at 6, maybe

more. The internal tussle continues, but finally common sense prevails. There are three rounds to go: "You're wounded, but don't make it fatal." I decide to play for a bogey 5, which means to the left of the bunker.

THE SHOT: It's still a tricky shot, and I give it maximum effort: an open blade, open stance, ball forward, very still with the head, a slow and easy, "fullish" swing with the left hand holding on firmly as the right makes the hit. The ball pops out perfectly and lands softly, stopping 15 feet from the hole. I barely miss the putt, and by the final round am well in the fight, but Gene Littler won't buckle. Disappointed as I am on the way home, I'm proud of my self-discipline in that first-round crisis. If I'd gone for the shot, I might never have had the fun even of contending.

THE LESSON: Never forget that success at stroke play very rarely depends on one shot. Disasters add to your psychic burden as well as your scorecard, so check any impulse to try for miracles short of a do-or-die situation on the final hole.

STAY AWAKE ON

2nd hole, par 5, 502 yards

THE SITUATION: It's the second hole of the final, and I'm all even with Dudley Wysong after routine opening pars. I've been playing all week about as well as I ever have, but, as always early in an important round, I'm nervous—and I want to settle down by drawing first blood. The second's a par 5, playing this day about 480 yards. A lot of people think it's a pretty mundane sort of straightaway hole, but I've learned better in earlier rounds. Distance-wise, I can reach it in two fairly easily off a decent drive, but the penalties for a bad off-line miss are severe. I've hit a good drive.

MY THOUGHT PROCESS: Dudley goes astray with a wood on his second shot and looks as if he could have trouble getting the ball close enough for a one-putt. It's raining, but the greens, as almost always at Pebble, are very firm. There's out-of-bounds close behind this one, and woods threatening left and rear, but the run in from the fairway is free of hazards. Adding it all up, I decide to try a low, hooked 2-iron.

THE SHOT: At address, I set the ball back about two inches nearer my right foot, close the clubface slightly and aim my feet, knees, hips and shoulders about 15 degrees right of where I want the ball to land. Going back, I swing the club on a path relative to my body alignment, *not* the direct target line, setting up an in-to-out path at impact. Coming down, I hit hard with a full release, plus a conscious effort to roll my right hand quickly over my left. The ball flies low, hot and nicely from right to left, but has a little bit too much steam and finally trickles off the green into a bunker. However, my next shot is an easy one compared with Dudley's. I pop the ball out to four feet, make the putt for a winning birdie and am on my way to my second U.S. Amateur victory.

THE LESSON: Never let a seemingly straightforward-looking hole lull you to sleep: *Always* observe, analyze, think and plan before you hit.

SLEEPY HOLES

**The 1962
U.S. Open
Championship**
Oakmont (Pa.) Country Club,

17th hole, par 4, 292 yards

A CRUCIAL CHIP

FROM TALL ROUGH

THE SITUATION: Tied with Arnold Palmer with two holes to play, I've tried to drive the green at the short 17th (since lengthened to 322 yards). The ball had the distance, but was pushed a hair, and finished wedged between grooves of sand in the right front bunker. From there I've played a heck of a shot that, if it had flown a foot farther, would have been up to the hole. However, I'm now in one of those U.S. Golf Association-patented collars of rough staring at a horrendous chip shot.

MY THOUGHT PROCESS: I'd figured birdie-par might make me the Open champion. Now I have to fight back the urge to second-guess myself about the go-for-broke tee shot. I just *know* I must make par here or it's *sayonara*. Somehow I force myself to bear down on what's now at hand. There's very little green to work with, and I'm staring at one of the toughest challenges in golf: Hit the ball hard enough to get it out of the rough, but not so hard that it goes way by the hole, or even clear through the green. It's a shot that has given me fits, but, thankfully, Art Wall had helped me enormously with it on the eve of the Open.

THE SHOT: Hold on very firmly with the left hand, Art recommended, open the clubface slightly, break the wrists sharply off the ball, then make a fairly full but slow—almost lazy—backswing. On the downswing, feel you're hitting against the firm left hand with the right while—and here's the key—*never speeding up the overall swing pace*. I apply the technique here, and the ball pops out cleanly, lands softly and rolls up four feet from the cup. I make the putt, par 18 and tie Arnie. I win the 18-hole playoff, 71-74.

THE LESSON: Be ready and eager to keep on learning everything you can about golf technique, and especially shots that have given you trouble, as this one had given me until Art supplied an answer. No one ever finds all the answers at golf, but it's fun trying— especially if you like winning.

IF YOUR NERVES

The 1962
U.S. Open Championship
Oakmont (Pa.) Country Club
17th hole, par 4, 292 yards

THE SITUATION: After that foolish go-for-the-green tee shot at 17, and a testy chip, I'm now only four feet from a par that will keep me tied with Arnold Palmer. But *what* a four-footer! First a break to the left, then almost at the hole a sharper turn to the right. And *fast*. Just thinking about that putt still gives me goose pimples!

MY THOUGHT PROCESS: I look the putt over for a long time, hoping to settle my nerves while trying to assess all the options. One is to attempt to read both breaks perfectly. Commit to a starting line, then try to "gentle" or "die" the ball into the hole. I'm not sure my pulse rate and adrenaline flow will let me make either the fine line judgment or the ultradelicate stroke necessary to do that. The only real alternative is to hit the ball straight and hard enough to eradicate both breaks—to ram it into the hole. Finally—going mostly, I guess, by what my nerves are telling me—that's my decision.

THE SHOT: There's a tremendous urge to rush very critical short putts, to get them over with, to release the almost unbearable tension. Usually, that's fatal. Somehow I force myself to set up very carefully, jiggling around until I'm certain about both my body alignment and the putterface: both dead square to the hole. Now the predominant thought becomes, "Stay still! Whatever happens, *stay still!*" As I begin to feel set, I take a couple of deep breaths for extra insurance, then fire. In my peripheral vision I see the ball begin straight for the hole, then hear it whang against the back and plunk to the bottom. A gush of relief floods through me. I hit my best drive of the week down 18, and 24 hours later I've won my first National Open and have my first professional victory.

THE LESSON: There are times when you just have to bite the bullet in golf and put all your faith in boldness. But, fight the tendency under extreme pressure to neglect the fundamentals before you pull the trigger.

TWITCH—DON'T BABY IT!

WHEN TO PLAY A DRIVE LIKE

THE SITUATION: With nine holes to go, I'm leading by two and feeling on top of the world. Less than an hour later, walking off the 12th green, I'm one back of Sam Snead and Gary Player, tied with Tony Lema and Julius Boros and thoroughly disgusted with myself. After three sloppy shots, only an eight-foot putt has saved me from making a double bogey on the shortest hole on the course. As I get to the 13th tee, I learn that Snead has birdied the 15th and is now two shots ahead.

MY THOUGHT PROCESS: Augusta National's 13th, at 475 yards, is what I think of as a marvelous "par 4½." At that distance, it offers at least a birdie, and in any final Masters round when I'm contending I feel I must make one here to stay in the race. On the other hand, there's disaster all around on every shot from even a slight miscue. For me, the key to a birdie or better is the tee shot. It must finish far enough around the dogleg to leave no more than a long iron from a reasonably level lie and approach angle, otherwise the

AN APPROACH

creek becomes too great a hazard to go for the green in two. For maximum control, I'd usually hit a 3-wood from the tee. Now I tell myself this is no time for faintheartedness. It has to be the driver.

THE SHOT: I'm having trouble shaking off the shock of the 12th hole, and the danger at times like this is to abbreviate the next swing by rushing it. I tell myself "Stay loose at address, set the club fully at the top and start down only as fast as you swung back." I align for the necessary draw: shoulders, hips, knees and feet slightly right, clubface fractionally closed. To minimize tension build-up, I begin the swing the moment I feel properly set up—no last-second delay or second-guessing. The shot turns out exactly as I've planned and visualized it. I hit the 2-iron to the green, two-putt for birdie and am right back in the thick of things. I go on to win by a stroke over Tony Lema.

The 1963 Masters Tournament
Augusta National Golf Club, Augusta, Ga.
13th hole, par 5, 475 yards

THE LESSON: Never treat tee shots more lightly than the strokes that seem to more heavily influence your score—and especially when you're "hot." How you put the ball in play is as big a factor as how well you hole out. The "just-haul-off-and-fire" tee-shot approach very rarely produces winners.

THE BREAKS WILL EVEN OUT—

THE SITUATION: My drive at the 15th in the final round is straight and long but finishes unluckily. I find the ball in a shallow divot mark, and, even worse, tight against a small tuft of dry turf. I'm one shot back of Sam Snead and desperately need to go for the green and make a birdie. Trouble is, any second shot coming up short or going long and left of the green will be swallowed by the water.

MY THOUGHT PROCESS: Given a good lie, I'd hit a regular 1-iron, but this club is too light-headed and straight-bottomed to dig the ball out of the divot and force it through the fronting crust of turf. An option is to lay up and try to pitch and putt for birdie, but wedge play isn't my strongest suit. Finally, I decide to go with the 3-wood. It's a high-risk shot, but I'm not interested in second place.

THE SHOT: I choke down a little on the 3-wood, and set up for a touch of fade in the hope of a softer landing and less roll—body aimed slightly left, clubface a little open. I make good contact, but the turf affects the spin of the ball. Instead of starting left and sliding high right, it shoots low left then hooks more left.· "There she goes, another Masters!" I say to myself, sure as I watch the ball vanish beyond the green that it's headed for the pond at the 16th. But there's no crowd groan, which indicates I've received one of my all-time great breaks. The course is soggy, spectators have left muddy tracks and the goo stops the ball short of the water. After a free drop, I play a great little 7-iron bump-and-run shot

to tour feet, and, even though I miss the putt, go on to win my first Masters by a stroke from Tony Lema.

THE LESSON: The breaks may not often even out for you on just one hole, as they did for me in this case, but in golf they always do over the long haul. Remembering that will help your sanity so your mind, rather than your emotions, will continue to function after a rough break.

EVENTUALLY

The 1963 Masters Tournament
Augusta (Ga.) National Golf Club

15th hole, 500 yards, par 5

BE CAREFUL WHEN YOU ARE

PUMPED UP

THE SITUATION: Bobby Jones made the 17th at Royal Lytham famous by "greening" a 175-yard mashie (5-iron) from sand and going on to win his first British Open in 1926. Leading by one over Bob Charles and Phil Rodgers, I'm standing in the fairway of this rugged par 4 after a sweet 3-wood tee shot, trying to figure what club to hit. I'm 10 yards short of where I'd driven in the third round that morning, when my 3-iron came up 25 feet short of the pin.

MY THOUGHT PROCESS: I'd played like a dog in my first attempt at the world's oldest golf championship the previous year, and want to win this time so badly I can taste it. Now, after rechecking the yardages, the shot is obvious: a smooth 2-iron.

THE SHOT: The long irons are my favorite clubs, and my swing is in the groove, so I feel totally confident. I set the ball behind a little to promote impact just as the clubhead reaches the bottom of its arc, and thus clip the ball cleanly off the hard, close-cropped links turf. Then the regular action: a one-piece start, good extension, full turn, complete the backswing, move to the left side and let her rip. The ball is hit purely, stung, but it lands beyond the hole and races into some wiry rough, from where I wedge poorly and two-putt for bogey. What I've forgotten is the effect of adrenaline, which, when you're contending, grows in inverse ratio to the number of holes remaining. The bogey contributes to an immediate further mental lapse at the final hole, and my weeklong dream stays just that. Charles defeats Rodgers in the 36-hole playoff, 140 to 148.

The 1963 British Open Championship
Royal Lytham and St. Annes Golf Club
Lancashire, England

17th hole, par 4, 427 yards

THE LESSON: Given that you make solid contact with the ball, the more "up" you are, the farther you'll hit every *full-swing* shot by pure reflex. So keep reminding yourself, as the adrenaline rises, to include this factor in all club-selection computations.

The 1963 British Open Championship
Royal Lytham and
St. Annes Golf Club
Lancashire, England

18th hole, par 4

A LITTLE DOUBT

WILL DO YOU IN

THE SITUATION: It's the fourth round, and I'm standing on the 18th tee trying to figure out whether I need a par to win or could still do so with a bogey. Challengers Bob Charles and Phil Rodgers are up on the 16th green, where I'd birdied, and I've been listening for crowd reactions indicating that either or both of them have done the same. I've heard nothing significant as it becomes time to hit.

MY THOUGHT PROCESS: I've been very confident all week, and therefore more relaxed and chatty on the course than normal. It will later transpire that this hasn't helped my arithmetic. Short of Phil or Bob birdieing 17 or 18, which is a tall order, I *think* I can make a bogey and still win, but am not absolutely sure. Anyway, the proper tee shot is crystal clear. The wind is left to right, so I should aim for the farthest bunker on the left edge of the fairway and let a slight left-to-right fade and the breeze blow the ball into position A.

THE SHOT: Immediately before leaving for England I'd regrooved my old bread-and-butter fade after a long spell of basically drawing the ball, and the left-to-right pattern hasn't failed me all week. I'm sure it won't now, but I set up as carefully as ever, the key to "working" the ball either way. Feet, knees, hips, shoulders aligned on the bunker, clubface fractionally open, establishing the slightly out-to-in swing path relative to the direct target line necessary to impart a little left-to-right sidespin. And it's all going fine until about two feet before impact, when my right hand suddenly jumps in, closing the clubface. The ball hooks into the bottom of a deep, steep-faced bunker. I discover that Bob and Phil both birdied 16, and I make bogey to lose by a stroke and have a *very* miserable trip home.

THE LESSON: Uncertainty about anything, and particularly something as critical as how you stand in a tournament, can do you in, even though it may only be subconscious. So try your darndest to eliminate doubts before every swing.

FEELING GOOD?

The 1963 PGA Championship
Dallas (Tex.)
Athletic Club

1st hole,
521 yards, par 5

COMPLETE THE BACKSWING

DON'T HOLD BACK!

THE SITUATION: Nine days previously I've given away a championship I thought I would win, the British Open at Royal Lytham & St. Annes, by bogeying the last two holes. There we'd played in two, sometimes three, sweaters. In Dallas, the temperature has rarely dropped below 110 degrees since we've gotten off the plane from England, and the heat seems to have burned away my usual major-championship resolve. For three days I've been pretty much just going through the motions. But, with the hangover of good form I'd taken into the British, I'm still only three strokes behind Bruce Crampton with 18 holes to play.

THE THOUGHT PROCESS: The day before the championship, I'd won a long-driving contest with a belt of 341 yards 17 inches. Now, finishing my warm-up with the driver before the final round, I figure I'm hitting the ball at least that far. My swing feels as great as the shots it's producing, so as I move to the practice putting green, I give myself a little pep talk: "Everyone's hurting from the heat, but you're in the groove and you can definitely win this thing. What you need is a strong start, and you've got a perfect opportunity with the opening par-5 hole."

THE SHOT: I get first-tee jitters like everyone else and, just like everyone else, the usual effect is to make me rush my swing because of the dreaded get-it-over-with-quick-and-get-out-of-here syndrome. This time, while selecting my aiming point and setting up to the shot, I make a special effort not to hurry by completing all the various little tasks and checkpoints extra-deliberately. Finally, ready to pull the trigger, I switch my mind to my No. 1 key swing thought, "Complete the backswing," and fire. When I get to the ball I figure out I have driven it slightly more than 350 yards. I choose the 5-iron for my second shot, hit it to 15 feet, then make the putt for an eagle 3 that gives me a super mental charge. Four hours later, still riding it, I've won my first PGA Championship.

THE LESSON: Opening a round conservatively is probably the best policy when you are not in top form, but when everything is meshing perfectly don't hesitate to be aggressive right from the bell. How do you determine the condition of your game? By warming up properly on the practice tee, of course.

The 1965
Masters Tournament
Augusta (Ga.) National
Golf Club,
2nd hole, par 5,
555 yards

LISTEN UP—TO

SOMEONE IN THE KNOW

THE SITUATION: I was so worried about my tee-to-green game as I practiced at Augusta the week ahead of the Masters that I flew down to Miami Beach for a session with Jack Grout. He helped, but the next day, back at Augusta, something else had gone wrong. I was spraying shots all over Georgia. About halfway through the round, pal Deane Beman, always a great diagnostician, offered a suggestion. Bingo! Now, after 37 holes of excellent golf, I'm tied with Arnold Palmer and Gary Player. I'm also 20 yards off the fairway right and deep in the piney woods.

MY THOUGHT PROCESS: You're always looking for a birdie at this hole, thus a bogey is pretty dispiriting. This time it would have been even more so because I'd gotten *two* lucky breaks: a good lie and a decent-size opening through the trees. So long as I kept the ball fairly low, I should be able to get close enough to the green for a pitch and possible one-putt. I did some figuring about height relative to distance and decided on the 3-iron.

THE SHOT: Deane had noticed that just before I started back I was closing my shoulders and hips slightly, which got the club too much to the inside. The result was that, unable to release properly, I either blocked the ball right—as on the drive here—or hooked it left. I'd been keying on the antidote for a week—a straight-back one-piece takeaway—but had let my concentration slip after having to wait a spell on the tee. "That's the last time," I told myself. I nailed the 3-iron, holed a good putt for birdie, and went on to shoot as near perfect a round as I ever have for a record-tying 64.

THE LESSON: When a knowledgeable golfer who knows your game thinks he's spotted a flaw, listen hard. My record wouldn't be anywhere near so satisfying if I hadn't had friends like Jack Grout, Deane Beman and Phil Rodgers, or listened very carefully when other pals on the tour thought they might have something to offer.

NO TIME FOR HEROICS

THE SITUATION: It's the final round and I'm waiting to hit at No. 12, Augusta National's most worrisome hole—maybe the most dangerous short par 3 in golf. The day before I had tied Lloyd Mangrum's 25-year-old course-record 64 to lead by five shots, and now, at 15 under par, I'm ahead by seven. Ben Hogan's 14-under-par 274 in 1953 is the 72-hole Masters record, and there has been a lot of speculation about a new one after my Saturday round.

MY THOUGHT PROCESS: Then as now, I'm *win*-conscious much more than *record*-conscious. It would tickle me to break the old record for four rounds, but that's secondary to finishing first. And, even with so big a lead, in my mind victory is by no means locked up—not with No. 12 still to be navigated and water on half of the remaining six holes. Record or no record, this is no time or place for heroics. The flagstick, as usual on the final day, is tucked lethally behind the right bunker. "Just make 3," I tell myself. "Just knock it in the heart of the green."

THE SHOT: The smaller the target you give yourself, the more pressure you place on setup and swing mechanics, which builds tension, which inhibits freedom of motion. If I elected to go for the pin, my target would be about a 10-foot circle around it. By deciding to play for the fat of the green, I more than double the "safe area." And, although I can get home with a hard 9-iron, I further ease the screws by going with a smooth 8-iron. I make an unpressured swing and super contact, drop the ball 25 feet from the hole, luck-in the putt for an unexpected bonus, go on to clip Ben's record by three strokes and win my second Masters by nine.

THE LESSON: Don't be a hero when you don't have to be. Play first to win, which means figuring and playing the percentages, and concern yourself with ancillaries like low scores or records only after you're certain of victory.

The 1965 Masters
Augusta (Ga.) National Golf Club
12th hole, par 3, 155 yards

GO WITH SHOTS

The 1966 Masters Tournament
Augusta National Golf Club
Augusta, Ga.

15th hole, par 5, 500 yards

THAT 'FEEL' THE BEST

THE SITUATION: With five holes to play, my chances of becoming the first golfer to defend successfully at Augusta appear slim to none. I've putted and concentrated poorly all week and am now three strokes behind Gay Brewer and two back of Tommy Jacobs. Now I've hit my drive at the par-5 15th in the worst possible place—behind the two pine trees on the left side of the fairway.

MY THOUGHT PROCESS: On 14, after hitting a tree from the tee, I've made my purest strike of the tournament, a nailed 3-iron that rolled up the roller-coaster green to within six feet of the hole. It boosts my confidence as I study the present situation. A birdie is mandatory, which spells "go for the green." There's just barely room to do so with a fade, but if the ball doesn't turn enough I can picture it bouncing through the hard left side of the green into the lake in front of the 16th tee. The safer shot, at least keeping the ball dry if the curvature doesn't come off perfectly, is a draw around the other side of the trees. Also, this is the better "feeling" shot at the moment. I decide to attempt it with the 2-iron.

THE SHOT: The more you seek to "finesse" the ball, the more imperative it becomes to build in the desired patterns with your setup. I have two goals with the flight of this shot: a strong draw to avoid the trees yet find the green, and a high trajectory to promote a softer landing. Always careful at address, I take extra care this time about aligning my body sufficiently right while positioning the ball where the clubhead will throw it highest by catching it at the exact bottom of the arc. Then, once set, I switch my mind to the word "release," because without free, fast clubhead application, a draw or hook is impossible. The shot comes off perfectly, I make my birdie and go on to tie Gay and Tommy (and win the playoff).

THE LESSON: When you're under the gun and have options, always go with shots that "look" the best in your mind's eye.

THANK YOU, TELEVISION

THE SITUATION: Gay Brewer, Tommy Jacobs and I have tied after 72 holes. My putting has ranged from average to awful all week and I'm just about to leave the clubhouse to work on it yet again when CBS replays me not even touching the hole from 3½ feet for birdie at the 17th—a miss that cost me an outright victory. Suddenly my putting clouds evaporate. I almost jog to the practice green.

MY THOUGHT PROCESS: One reason I've spent so much time over the years with my teacher, Jack Grout, is that a player can't see himself at this game. You may *think* you know what you're doing wrong, but usually you're just guessing. And when a problem becomes really persistent it's awfully easy to overexperiment into even greater trouble. To avoid that, and to save time, my answer has always been to enlist Grout's eagle eye and great knowledge of my methods. In this case, fortuitously, television did the same job for me.

THE SHOT: My problem on 17—in fact, all week

—was my eye alignment at address. There aren't many hard and fast rules about putting as I see it, but one of them is to set up with your eyes directly over the ball, and therefore directly over the line along which you need to start the ball. If you don't, you'll have one heck of a job squaring the putter to the actual line you've chosen. If your eyes are inside the ball, you'll tend to aim the face to the right of the correct line. In this instance, I was doing the opposite: eyes out beyond the ball, making me aim the putterface to the left of the line I'd identified when reading the putt from directly behind the ball. As soon as I repositioned my eyes directly over the ball, everything fell into place. I did not hit one bad putt the next day, and at the end of the playoff became the first man to help himself into a green jacket, winning back-to-back Masters.

THE LESSON: When some element of your game goes sour, and you can't put a finger on the cause within a short period of time, swallow your pride and obtain help from a professional.

**The 1966
Masters Tournament**
Augusta (Ga.) National Golf Club
17th hole, par 4, 400 yards

THE SITUATION: Third round. I've given away the lead on the opening hole, and am fighting getting down on myself. This is the year of ribbon fairways through thigh-high rough, and I've stuck with the 1-iron or 3-wood for most tee shots. The fifth is an exception because of its birdie potential, and I need the boost a birdie would bring. I nail the driver, but then let the 7-iron hang a little too far right. The ball kicks down into soft sand.

TIME TO BE BOLD

The 1966 British Open Championship

The Honourable Company of Edinburgh Golfers (Muirfield), Gullane, Scotland 5th hole, par 5, 516 yards

MY THOUGHT PROCESS: I stay cool because, given the ground contour, pin placement and wind direction, this is the place to be if you miss the green. But the upcoming shot calls for great delicacy, and bunker play hasn't exactly been my strongest suit. I'm determined not to give away the birdie. I take plenty of time thinking out the stroke, and finally decide to risk a special splash technique I've recently been working on. I don't figure on flubbing it, but the fact that I can still make par if I don't get the ball as close as I'd like influences my decision.

THE SHOT: I need the ball to fly softly and land stone dead. It won't do that with a regular explosion shot, but I've found I can get the effect by simply picking the club up and dropping it in back of the ball without a follow-through—much like playing a buried ball, but without the force. I set up with the ball well forward in my open stance, and open the clubface wide for maximum loft. I swing back fairly long but nice and easy, then simply drop the clubhead into the sand under the ball about an inch in back and let it stop. The ball pops gently out and flops dead by the hole, and I get a tap-in birdie and the necessary charge.

THE LESSON: Pick your moments to try high-risk shots. In this case I could still have made par if I messed up a little, and there were still 31 holes to play in the championship. If I'd been risking bogey or worse, or things had been tighter, I'd likely have played more conservatively.

The 1966
British Open

The Honourable
Company of
Edinburgh Golfers
Muirfield, Scotland

17th hole, par 5,
528 yards

CONSULT YOUR

'COMPUTER,' THEN HIT

THE SITUATION: In the third round, I'd been sailing along merrily, well in the lead, when the wheels fell off. Playing jittery golf, I'd bogeyed four of the last five holes to end the day two shots back of Phil Rodgers. On the front nine of the final round, I'd restored my lead and my confidence. Then I missed a seven-foot putt for birdie at 11, *and* the 15-inch tap-in, and followed with two more bogeys and a couple of very wobbly pars. Finally, at the 16th, as my first solidly stroked putt since the 11th almost dropped for birdie, I began to regain some composure. Now I'm standing by my tee shot on the 17th fairway.

MY THOUGHT PROCESS: The hole is a 528-yard par 5, playing downwind with rock-hard ground. At the tee I'd forced my mind off thoughts of a playoff and onto what I needed to win outright—a birdie and a par. I'd then hit a solid 3-iron that left me 238 yards to the center of the green. Now, with slim chance of birdie at the tough 18th, I just *have* to select the right club. I fight the urge to rush the decision in favor of a step-by-step analysis

THE SHOT: For me, under normal conditions, 238 yards calls for the 1-iron. OK, start from there and *think.* I'm playing the smaller British ball, which flies farther, so take off one club. A big wind at my back, so take off, say, one and a half clubs more. Hard ground, lots of run—that's down another full club. And don't forget how charged up I am, which means I'll give it that little bit more oomph—say half a club more. So that's one, one and a half, one, and a half, which adds up to four clubs less than normal, which equals the 5-iron. Certain that the computation is as sound as I can make, I take the 5-iron, produce a confident swing, strike the ball perfectly, make a two-putt birdie, and win my first British Open by a stroke when I par the final hole.

THE LESSON: Know how far you regularly hit each iron, figure how far you have to go on all approaches, and put that computer in your head in high gear whenever conditions are abnormal.

The 1966 British Open Championship
The Honourable Company of Edinburgh Golfers (Muirfield), Gullane, Scotland
18th hole, par 4, 427 yards

HOW TO KEEP

COOL UNDER PRESSURE

THE SITUATION: Dave Thomas and Doug Sanders have finished the tournament at 283. After 71 holes, I need a par for 282. The 18th at Muirfield is one of the toughest finishing holes on the British Open rota, demanding distance plus great accuracy. I'm a little tempted to hit a wood off the tee, but stick with my weeklong game plan to avoid the knee-high hay and go with a 1-iron. My tee shot puts me in ideal position for the second shot.

MY THOUGHT PROCESS: All I'm after is getting within certain two-putt range—no heroics. My yardage chart shows I'm 208 yards from the heart of the green. The pin is tucked left and to miss it on that side could be "deadsville." So could being too long. The wind, blowing briskly from the right, has provided a perfect bank for my natural fade on the tee shot. I figure it should do the same again. But what club? The little voice inside keeps saying, "4-iron," but something makes me hesitate. I will have to swing hard and get every bit of the ball. Finally, I say to heck with that at a moment like this and haul out the 3-iron.

THE SHOT: Adrenaline makes you want to powder the ball, and it promotes that tendency in the muscles. As I set up for the fade—clubface slightly open, body aimed a little left—I lock in on the word "smooth." My target is the center of the green. The impact feels magical; as solid a strike as I've ever made. And the wonderful feeling continues as I watch the ball start left, then soar up and hold its line perfectly against the wind, finally dropping like a butterfly, hole-high and about 25 feet right of the flag. A lag and a tap-in later, I sort of conk out emotionally for a few minutes. Not only have I finally captured a major championship that I secretly feared might always evade me, but have won all four of them at least once. I'm one happy guy.

THE LESSON: Resist the tendency to play too quickly under pressure and give yourself extra thinking time when your adrenaline is gushing hardest. The urge is to go with your instincts and take less club on approaches, but then you have to meet the ball squarely for the shot to succeed. Smoothness with plenty of club is usually a better strategy.

ACCELERATE THE PUTTERHEAD

The 1967
U.S. Open

Baltusrol Golf Club,
Springfield, N.J.
4th hole, par 3,
194 yards

AND *HIT* THE BALL

THE SITUATION: Round two, fourth hole, the lovely but difficult 194-yard over-water par 3. I've missed the green left, gone to sleep on the chip, and now have an 11-foot putt to save par. After an opening three-putt bogey, I'm two over for the championship. Scoring is low, with nine guys under par in the first round and mostly moving well today. Drop another stroke here and, with the inevitable mental downer, I could hoist myself out of range by day's end.

MY THOUGHT PROCESS: It had been an awful year, my longest and worst slump since turning pro, chiefly due to lousy putting. A 27-putt 62 in final practice, using a new putter and a different technique, seemed to have turned things around at last. Then, when we began for real, the magic vanished: 35 putts in the first round. But I thought I knew the reason: simply not enough time to build complete confidence in the new method, thus an insufficiently decisive stroke. I'd been there before and knew there was only one answer. Willpower.

THE SHOT: I'd had a new putter for some days—a white-painted Bulls Eye lent me by Fred Mueller, a friend of Deane Beman. The new technique I'd gotten only the evening before my 62, courtesy of a pal from Ohio, Gordon Jones. Watching me miss from all over on the practice green, he'd suggested a shorter backswing and a more rapping hit. It was the exact opposite of what I'd been working on for weeks, but it was also how I'd putted so well as a kid, and it had helped immediately. Setting up now over that crucial 11-footer, I tell myself: "Just *believe* in it, will you? *Make* yourself take it back short, then *hit* it." The contact feels perfect, the ball drops clean, and the huge lift I get produces five more birdies that day and eight more in my final round 65 to beat Arnold Palmer by four shots and set a new Open 72-hole record of 275.

THE LESSON: If you're putting badly, it's easy to get so wrapped up in mechanics that you forget the No. 1 fundamental of all golf shots: *Strike the ball.* Acceleration through impact is a must, both to reach the hole and to keep the ball on line. Frequently, you'll find the easiest way to increase your acceleration is to shorten your backswing. As with any method change, you'll also need some peptalking and extra willpower at first.

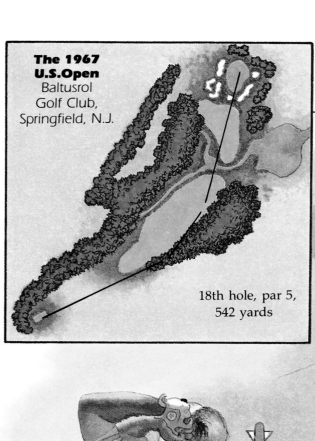

The 1967 U.S.Open
Baltusrol
Golf Club,
Springfield, N.J.

18th hole, par 5,
542 yards

LET PRIORITIES

DETERMINE STRATEGY

HOGAN 276
NICKLAUS 275

THE SITUATION: I'm playing with Arnold Palmer, and going into the final hole I'm leading him by four strokes. If I close with a birdie, I'll break Ben Hogan's 72-hole Open record, but the figure uppermost in my mind is 6. If I make no more than 6, I'm certain to win outright, even if Arnie makes an eagle 3. There is severe trouble on both sides of the fairway, and for some dumb reason the thought of Dick Mayer's double bogey off a poor tee shot here in 1954 (causing him to lose to Ed Furgol) keeps running through my mind. Finally, I decide on the 1-iron from the tee, hit it scruffy into the right rough, but get a free drop due to some nearby television equipment. Now I must lay up short of the water. I take the 8-iron, set up for a three-quarter punch shot, look up, hit the ground a couple of inches behind the ball and move it about 100 yards.

MY THOUGHT PROCESS: Arnold is just short of and to the right of the green in two. He could still make 3 by chipping in. My distance is 238 yards, but uphill, all carry and against the wind, which computes to more like 260 yards. That spells 3-wood, but I don't feel confident about hitting it straight enough. What I really like for maximum control is to hit a 2- or 3-iron. I do the math over again to see if I can make either of them fit. I can't. It has to be the 1-iron.

THE SHOT: The critical thing is to fly the hillside bunker in front of the green, a carry of about 220 yards. I've just made a couple of swings that wouldn't do that, so for insurance, I aim just left of the bunker, which, with a solid hit and a slight fade, ought to at least get me within reasonable two-putt range. I throw everything I own into the swing and push the ball just a fraction. But, oh boy, what contact! The ball carries the corner of the bunker, bounces just short of the green and rolls up 22 feet from the hole. I work hard on the putt and make it, giving me the record as well as a second U.S. Open title. But the shot to cherish is that 1-iron. I still don't believe I could have hit the ball that well or that far with that club.

THE LESSON: Let your priorities determine your strategies when you face hard decisions in club selection. My priority here was the title, and the extra confidence that came from choosing the right club produced a strong and aggressive swing that also set up a record.

The 1967 British Open

Royal Liverpool
Golf Club
Hoylake, England
16th hole, par 5,
529 yards

WHEN MY BEST

WASN'T GOOD ENOUGH

THE SITUATION: It is the final round, and the championship by this point is between Roberto De Vicenzo and me. My second shot has stopped a little short and right of the green, on the fairway, but on a patch so burned out it's like hardpan. There is a bunker smack in front of me and the pin is tucked tightly behind it.

MY THOUGHT PROCESS: Any kind of regular pitch would send the ball well past the pin, making a birdie unlikely, but a par pretty certain. If I were ahead, or even tied, that would be the percentage play. Now it simply won't do. I *must* make a birdie to increase the pressure on Roberto, and that calls for a high-risk touch shot. I rehearse the technique in my mind, and then a number of times with the swing, very conscious that Byron Nelson, doing TV commentary, is watching close by. I'm not exactly fa-

mous for skill with the wedges. Byron's presence is an extra incentive not to mess up.

THE SHOT: The technique I've decided on is similar to a gentle bunker shot, and there are three keys to it. The first is a slow, full, soft swing. The second is dropping the clubhead in slightly behind the ball so that the face slides or skids beneath it. The third and most important is positioning the face of the sand wedge so that just a little of the bounce comes into play, which means square to very slightly open with the shaft vertical rather than angled forward toward the target. I'm extra meticulous in setting up this way, then make exactly the swing I've pictured. The flange of the club meets the ground about an inch behind the ball, the face slides nicely under and the ball stops two and a half feet from the hole. I make the putt and birdie 18, but it doesn't matter. Roberto finishes strongly for a popular victory by two shots.

THE LESSON: This technique will save you a bunch of strokes from rough and sand as well as from the fairway, but it takes confidence and thus needs plenty of practice. Pay particular attention to establishing the proper degree of bounce via the clubface alignment at address. Too little and you'll stick the leading edge in the ground. Too much and you'll blade the ball. Experiment to get it right.

The 1968 British Open
Carnoustie Golf Club, Carnoustie, Scotland

18th hole, par 5, 525 yards

LEARN TO DRAW

The right way

THE BALL

THE SITUATION: Last round, and I'm paired with pal Gary Player. It's been a dogfight since the turn. I'm two strokes back. I birdie 14, Gary eagles it. I make a solid par at 15, Gary gets up and down from 100 yards to match me. At the 243-yard, par-3 16th, I nail a career driver into the wind and pick up a stroke. At 17 I drive more than 350 yards but don't capitalize with the pitch, and Gary almost holes out from 70 feet—two pars. I hit another great drive into the wind at 18. Playing the percentages, Gary goes safely from the tee but then half-hits his second into tall grass 140 yards short of the pin. He's still leading me by two. I could win outright with an eagle, or send us into overtime with a birdie.

MY THOUGHT PROCESS: The Barry Burn fronts the green and there's out-of-bounds tight left, but I put them both out of mind—this is no time for caution. The pin is at the rear of the green 240 yards away, and the wind is dead against me. I don't want to risk the 3-wood, but I know I can't get the ball all the way back with a straight 1-iron. I decide to aim at the bunker right of the green and draw the ball, relying on the extra run to get it to the hole.

THE SHOT: I feel confident about moving the ball from right to left, but am extra meticulous in setting up for the correct amount of curve: body aligned slightly right, clubface fractionally toed-in. The backswing feels fine, but coming down my upper body moves just a little ahead of the ball and I can't release fully. I get the distance but not the curve, finishing in the bunker I've aligned with. Gary plays a great third shot, two-putts for par, and wins his second British Open.

THE LESSON: Most amateurs, and especially short hitters, would improve their games immeasurably by learning to draw the ball consistently. Producing that flight requires complete release of the clubhead before the hands get ahead of the ball, and the key to that is staying well behind the ball through impact. Setting your head back of the ball, then concentrating on keeping it there, will help you do that

FIND YOUR FEEL

The 1970
British Open
Championship

The Old Course,
St. Andrews, Scotland
18th hole,
par 4, 358 yards

IN REHEARSAL

THE SITUATION: I've three-putted eight times in the third and fourth rounds, but a famous missed putt by Doug Sanders on the final hole of regulation play gives me a second chance. With four holes left in our playoff, I'm four strokes ahead, but then Doug gets hot. Standing on the 18th tee, watching his fine drive, my lead is down to one and my mind is on a birdie. The wind is at our backs and I decide to go for the green. I peel off a sweater, reach for the driver, and crush it. The ball races through the green and into some heavy grass about halfway up the bank behind it, only a few feet from out-of-bounds. Doug plays his pitch-and-run second to within about five feet of the hole.

MY THOUGHT PROCESS: Doug had started putting beautifully at 14, and I'm certain he won't make the previous day's mistake again. That means I need to get down in two to avoid sudden death. But I'm looking at a severe downhill lie to a slick, down-sloping green, with the Valley of Sin an eager receptacle if I'm a hair too strong. The only good part is that the long grass nestled around the ball slants toward the green, thus reducing my chance of snagging the club.

THE SHOT: Because I use it so much from around the green, my maximum-confidence club under the gun is the sand wedge. I pull it out and make a number of very careful practice swings, working on positioning my feet and hands at the precise points ahead of the ball that will promote swinging back and through parallel with the slope, and also on the weight of the stroke. Setting up for real, I tell myself, "Stay still" a couple of times, then swing. The ball pops out almost perfectly and rolls down eight feet short of the cup. When I make the putt, I jump about 10 feet in the air and let go of the putter, which almost brains poor Doug. I've finally won "The" Open at the Home of Golf, and the excitement is uncontrollable.

THE LESSON: Pros frequently don't make practice swings ahead of full shots, but you'll rarely see them play a little tester like this one without ample rehearsal. Be sure to give yourself enough time to find and lock in the "feel" of those critical short recovery strokes.

PUT YOUR MIND TO THE NEXT

THE SITUATION: Starting the final round with a four-stroke lead, I'm secretly convinced it's all over but the shouting. Sixteen holes later, I'm still two shots ahead of Billy Casper, but clean out of cockiness. I've made four bogeys and two birdies, with an awful lot of scrambling for the intervening pars. The 17th hole is a long par 5, and the 18th is among the hardest finishing holes in golf. I'm trying to decide what club to hit off the 17th tee.

MY THOUGHT PROCESS: The previous day I'd hit a driver, then had attempted to get home with a 3-wood and had been awfully lucky not to dunk the ball, stopping just inches from the water on the left. If I hit a driver now and nail it, I'll be very tempted to try for the green again. If I go with the 3-wood from the tee, there will be no chance of that. On the other hand, if I only make a par here and Bill birdies 18, I'll have to par that tough 18th to avoid a playoff. I think it through a couple of more times, then decide to go with my instincts—3-wood.

THE SHOT: Not concerned about distance, I make a fine swing and split the fairway. Then, as I walk off the tee, a big roar signals that Bill has done just what I figured he might—closed with a birdie. For a moment I can't help second-guessing myself. Now a par here might not be good enough. Have I goofed by laying back off the tee? Dwelling on a thought like that is poison. I force it out of my mind by turning my thoughts to calculating the yardage. Then I hit a 1-iron short of the bunkers in front of the green, follow with a nice wedge shot and a five-footer dead in the heart. After a pressureless par at 18, I become the only golfer to win all four majors at least twice.

THE LESSON: You're always going to have self-doubts, and they'll destroy your game if you let them gnaw at you. The answer lies in the inability of the brain to think hard about two things at once. Force your mind to the next challenge just as fast as you can and the bad pictures surely will vanish.

CHALLENGE

The 1971 PGA Championship
PGA National Golf Club, East Course
(Now the JDM Country Club)
Palm Beach Gardens, Fla.
17th hole, par 5, 588 yards

The 1971 U.S. Open
Merion Golf Club,
Ardmore, Pa.

11th hole, par 4, 370 yards

COMPLACENCY

THE SITUATION: I'm a couple of shots back after the first round, but am sailing along happily in the second just one stroke off the lead going to the 11th tee. I've won two tournaments and lost one in a playoff since the Masters, and I'm eager to make up for some giveaway golf there. I'm swinging well and putting well, and just love the golf course. All is right in my world.

MY THOUGHT PROCESS: The 11th at Merion is where Bob Jones closed out Gene Homans in the final of the 1930 U.S. Amateur to complete the Grand Slam. It's short, but the dog-legging off the tee, then Baffling Brook coiling around the green, make it tricky. Because Merion is like that most of the way—short but tricky—my game plan is to largely forgo the driver in favor of the 3-wood or 1-iron. This worked beautifully at Muirfield in the 1966 British Open, and it has worked fine for 28 holes this week, and I see no reason to forgo it now. One-iron, soft little fade into the center of the fairway, followed by a 9-iron or wedge pitch, and maybe a shot at a birdie. Easy game.

THE SHOT: I set up fine: body aligned on the left edge of the fairway, clubface slightly open. Starting back full of confidence, I immediately sense I've let the clubhead move beyond a line parallel with my shoulders—too much to the outside. Sometimes I can reroute the club a little coming down, and I try. No, sir. The ball slices into heavy rough, from where I scythe it into the right rough just short of the forest, from where I leave the wedge short, from where I hit a terrible chip through the green and down the bank almost into the Baffling Brook, from where I finally get to the putting surface and make a very shaky four-footer for a double-bogey 6. Forty-four holes later, Lee Trevino and I end up tied, and he beats me in the playoff.

THE LESSON: No matter how well you're playing and no matter how chipper you are about the outcome, don't ever take anything for granted. The gods of golf don't like complacent golfers. Make every swing with the thought that it's the one you need to win.

The 1972 Masters Tournament
Augusta (Ga.) National Golf Club,

11th hole, par 4, 455 yards

ALLOW A GREAT

SHOT TO SPUR YOU ON

THE SITUATION: Practicing the week before the Masters, I develop a tempo fault in my downswing leg action that throws out my iron game. Along with poor course conditions due to bad spring weather, this gets me off to a bad start in the tournament. After 10 holes, I've made three bogeys to one birdie, plus only two non-scrambling pars. I'm playing nervously and tentatively. But at 11, I suddenly hit a super drive.

MY THOUGHT PROCESS: This is the year the press seems to be asking not "Will Jack Nicklaus win the Grand Slam?" but "When?" That's adding to the pressure, but it's also a spur. Standing by my ball in the 11th fairway, I decide enough is enough. My yardages indicate a 5-iron. Normally, even with that short club, because of the water fronting almost the entire green I play to the right side for a safe two-putt par. I decide this time I'm going to make eagle 2.

THE SHOT: I take dead aim on the flag, located dangerously left of center but pretty deep in the green. The swing feels great and the ball covers the pin all the way. For a thrilling moment I think it might actually go in the hole. Instead, it stops 12 feet away. I give the putt a lot of work and a lot of willpower, and make it. At the 12th I hole from 25 feet for another birdie, and make it three in a row after a nice little sand shot at 13. I make a solid par at 14, then hit a drive and 1-iron to 30 feet at 15 and sink it for an eagle. At 16, I hole from 22 feet to go six under for six holes. The final tally is 68, and it gives me a cushion against most of the top names. I play some sloppy golf at times the next three days, but in the end win a record-tying fourth Masters by three strokes.

THE LESSON: Do your darndest to capitalize on a specially fine shot whenever your game isn't quite in sync. Such a shot signifies that you've still got what it takes, and that it could come back any moment. Even more important is the psychological pick-me-up of a well-played hole after a spell of scruffy golf. I doubt if I would have won this Masters without the hot streak triggered by that go-for-it birdie at 11 in the opening round.

EVEN A BOGEY CAN GIVE YOU

THE SITUATION: I have a three-stroke lead at the turn in the final round, but then double-bogey 10. Wind and lack of water have dried the course almost to the point of unplayability, and especially this always tough par 3. The ideal shot is a high, soft-landing fade with a long iron, but with the wind whistling across from the Pacific on the left, that isn't "on" today. I decide to hit the 3-iron, drawing the ball to hold it against the wind, and couldn't play a better shot if I stood there for a year. The ball lands dead on the stick and 10 feet short of it, but races on through the green and down the steep bank behind it. I leave the ultra-delicate pitch in rough at the top of the bank, then play what at first I think is a great shot, just popping the ball onto the green. But the surface is like glass, and the ball finally trickles to a stop eight feet past the hole.

MY THOUGHT PROCESS: There has never been a better year for me in terms of major championship courses. I've won the Masters, I've worked very hard preparing for this Open, and I've gotten myself in great position with nine holes to play.

Now I'm in real danger of giving it all away. "Come on," I tell myself, "you've just made one double bogey and you are *not* going to make another. Bear down, get with it, show some guts. You're upset and you're getting negative, but *you can make this putt.*"

THE SHOT: I take a lot of time reading the putt from all angles. The good news is that it will work a little—about half an inch—from right to left, for me, as for most golfers, the easier break. The bad news is the slipperiness of the surface and the strength of the wind ruffling both mind and body. "Don't rush it," I remind myself. "Get comfortable, wait until you are good and ready." It takes a lot of willpower, but I wiggle around until something says, "OK, go." I tap the ball *very* gently. As it gets about halfway to the hole, I know it's in, and I get a very big charge from watching it drop.

THE LESSON: Even after a recovery like this, many golfers would cuss themselves out for making a bogey. I got a lift, and the reason is that I work hard at staying realistic on a golf course. Under the prevailing conditions, a bogey was more than likely the best I could hope for. Never let your emotions rule your intellect in rough conditions.

A LIFT

**The 1972
U.S. Open**
Pebble Beach Golf Links,
Pebble Beach, Calif.

12th hole, par 3, 205 yards

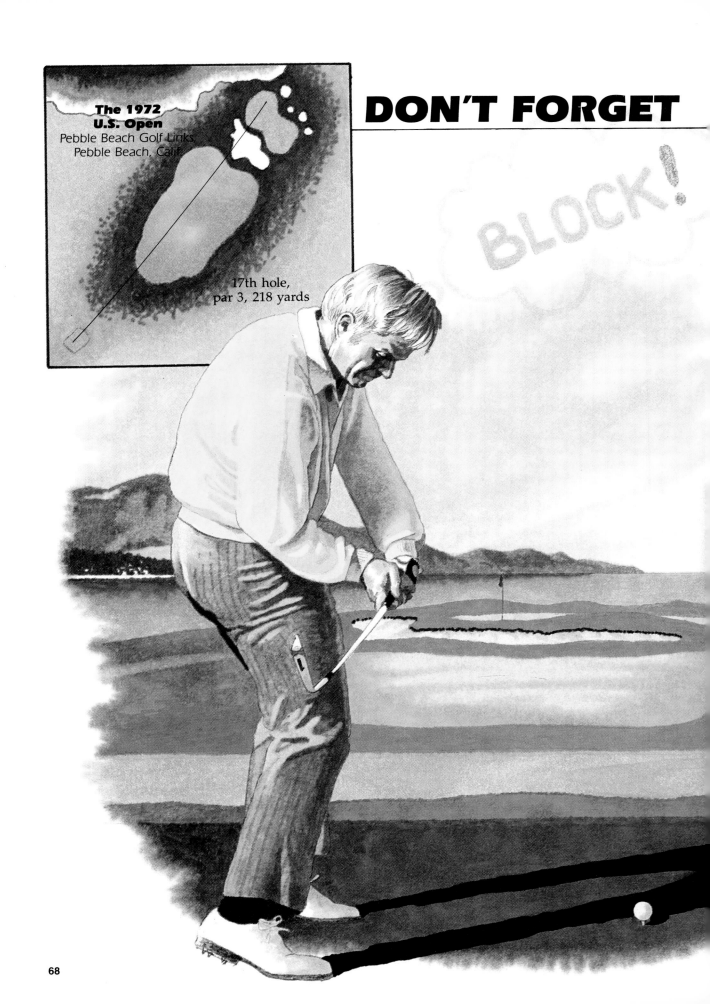

SOUND FUNDAMENTALS

THE SITUATION: I'm leading by three strokes with two holes to play. A few hours previously I've dreamed over and over that there is no way I can finish either of them, and especially 17 with the pin tight behind the bunker on the left side of the ridge that divides the figure-eight green. That's where it is, and, just as in the dream, the wind is howling in dead against me all the way from China.

MY THOUGHT PROCESS: Go for the pin and hook the ball and there's a strong likelihood I'll have a nasty encounter with the world's biggest water hazard. Bail out right and, even if I hit the green or fringe, I'll need a miracle shot to get close enough for a chance at par. I say to heck with that and reach for the 1-iron. Dream or no dream, a three-stroke lead is a three-stroke lead. Also, I've been swinging beautifully all day.

THE SHOT: I take dead aim on the flag, but, starting back, knowing I need all the distance the club can give me and involuntarily protecting against a fade, I feel myself closing the clubface and working a little too much inside the target line. That spells hook, but my tempo has never been better and now it produces one of the finest shots of my career. Coming down I'm able to "block" or delay the clubhead release just sufficiently to deliver the face square to the ball, but without significant loss of speed. The ball bores through the wind low and dead on the stick. I can't see it land but a big roar tells me it's close. When I get up there it's two inches from the hole, and someone tells me it hit the stick and almost fell in for an ace. A few minutes later I've won a third U.S. Open and am half way to the modern Grand Slam.

THE LESSON: A correct setup to the ball—grip, clubface aim, body alignment, posture—is 80 percent of good shotmaking. Get the backswing initiated correctly and you've covered almost all of the remaining 20 percent. I was lucky on this shot, but that didn't stop me putting in some solid work on the above fundamentals in the ensuing weeks.

DON'T GET CAUGHT PLAYING

THE SITUATION: With two legs of the Grand Slam under my belt, I get to Scotland in time for seven practice rounds. I'm very happy about my game starting the championship, but after 54 holes I'm six shots in back of Lee Trevino and five adrift of Tony Jacklin. Over-influenced by my conservative winning strategy at Muirfield six years previously, I've played the now less-punitively prepared course too cautiously. Finally going for everything in the last round, I reach six under par and am leading by a stroke with three holes to play.

MY THOUGHT PROCESS: The crowds are rooting for me like never before and I'm pumped to the gills and bursting with confidence. I'm not exactly counting my chickens, but I'm playing and putting so well, and on such a roll, that thoughts of failure simply don't enter my mind. I figure that a par at 16, a birdie at the par-5 17th and a par to finish—the same 3-4-4 finish I had in 1966—and I'm only one step away from a lifelong dream.

THE SHOT: Sixteen is a medium-length par 3 to a long, skinny, elevated green. I want to leave the ball short of the pin—under the hole for an uphill putt. I have no doubts about the club: a solid 4-iron. I make what feels like an excellent swing, but pull the shot just a hair. The ball hits on the front of the green, but

kicks almost sideways and trickles into some thickish rough. I play as good a pitch as I'm capable of from such a lie to six feet beyond the hole. I read the putt to break an inch and a half from right to left, and hit it exactly as I intend. It breaks down much faster than I've figured and never even touches the hole. The bogey is my only one of the day, but, shaken, I hit a bad drive at 17 and can't make a birdie. Lee Trevino later hits a poor drive at 17, but holes a pitch-and-run from over the green for a par and wins by one stroke.

THE LESSON: Golf can be a heartbreaking game, and this was my No. 1 heartbreaker. What caused it was living in the past instead of the here and now. Muirfield as set up in 1972 called for a different strategy than in 1966, but I was either not smart enough or too stubborn to see that until I'd backed myself into a corner. Use your past experience, but never let it blind you to present conditions.

IN THE PAST

The 1972 British Open
The Honourable Company of Edinburgh Golfers (Muirfield), Gullane, Scotland

16th hole, 188 yards, par 3

The 1973 Masters Tournament
Augusta (Ga.) National Golf Club,

15th hole, par 5, 520 yards

LET ONE

MISTAKE STOP RIGHT THERE

THE SITUATION: After trailing by a stroke at the end of the first round, I three-putt eight times for a horrendous 77 in the second. In round three, still fighting my putter, I scrape and scramble to one under par through 14. I hit a big drive at 15, but the ball just catches the top of one of the mounds on the right side of the fairway and rolls back about halfway down the slope.

MY THOUGHT PROCESS: A birdie here and I'm back to even par for the tournament, and only a couple of shots off the lead. I have 250 yards to the front of the green. The ball is sitting pretty well, but the lie is uphill. The safe play is a lay-up short of the water, but I'd need an exceptional pitch to stop the ball within one-putt range. I decide to go for the green. Because of the extra height and shorter carry produced by an uphill lie, it has to be the 3-wood.

THE SHOT: The trick with uphill and downhill lies is to set the body at address as perpendicular to the slope as possible, so that the path of the clubhead through impact equates to the angle of incline. The problem with that is making a complete backswing from what inevitably feels like an uncomfortably restricted setup. I fail to do so, and catch the ball thin. It splashes into the pond a few feet short of the far bank. I walk down and drop another ball short of the water under penalty of one stroke. It rolls into a depression and I hit the pitch fat. Splash! I get the next one on the green and two-putt for a triple-bogey 8. The next day I close with an eight-birdie 66, but it leaves me two strokes light of Tommy Aaron.

THE LESSON: I committed the high handicapper's principal sin here: turning one slip into a disaster through lack of patience. If I'd played smart on the second shot, or simply hit the first pitch somewhere on the green and two-putted, I'd have made 6, which, as it turned out, would have put me in a playoff. Instead, I got greedy and tried to do too much relative to the lie twice in a row, and I paid a heavy price. I'm sure you know the feeling!

MY HOMEWORK PAYS OFF

THE SITUATION: Fighting low scores as always, the Oakmont authorities have added 27 yards to the 322-yard 17th hole for the championship, plus some new trees on top of the hill in front of the green. The theory is the hole can no longer be driven. After going back out there and hitting some balls following my final practice round, I figure that's wrong. Now's my chance to prove it. I'm two over par in the opening round, and the wind, usually against you here, is behind and from the right.

MY THOUGHT PROCESS: The regular play is a fairway wood or long iron out to the right side of the fairway, followed by a little pitch. The greens are slick and crusty and I figure I'll have difficulty holding this green directly downwind, even with a flip wedge. Carrying the trees is no problem, so the worst I should have if I miss the putting surface is a sand or chip shot. Also, I need a lift—badly. I haul out the driver.

THE SHOT: As I'm lining up, I hear my playing partner, Bob Goalby, mutter to a marshal: "Boy, if that's not a dumb shot!" It strengthens my resolve and I make an excellent swing. The ball takes off dead on the direct line, and as it vanishes over the hill I say, "That's on the green." When I get up there I learn the ball landed a few feet short of the putting surface, hopped once and rolled on. It's 12 feet short of the cup, and I make the putt for an eagle 2. Bob meanwhile has played the orthodox way, but has to work hard for his par. Walking off he complains about that, and we both get a big laugh when I tell him, "Well, that's because you played a dumb shot from the tee!" Three days later Johnny Miller wins his first major with a sensational 63, but the lift I've received from driving that "undrivable" hole helps to keep me in the hunt almost to the end.

THE LESSON: Carefully evaluating the percentages ahead of time adds to your competitive armory. By going out and hitting some drivers the evening before the championship, I'd discovered that what seemed a high-risk shot actually wasn't, given a helping wind. The card may have said 322 yards, but the direct route was only 270, which was well within my carrying capability. Knowing that allowed me to make a confident golf swing.

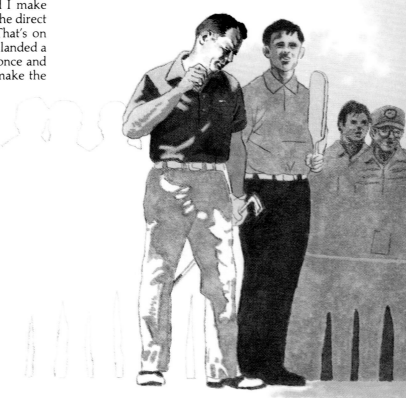

The 1973 U.S. Open
Oakmont (Pa.)
Country Club
17th hole, par 4, 322 yards

The 1973 PGA Championship

Canterbury Golf Club, Cleveland, Ohio 14th hole, par 4, 385 yards

MAKE THE NATURAL CHOICE

THE SITUATION: I'm playing with Bruce Crampton, my closest challenger two strokes back, as we reach the 14th hole in the final round. Like so many of the par 4s at Canterbury, this one calls for precision from the tee along with good distance. Accordingly, I take the 3-wood, but push it into the right rough. Bruce surprises me by going with the driver and hooks it badly, almost out-of-bounds.

MY THOUGHT PROCESS: This is my last opportunity of the season to win a major, and if I do so I

exceed Bob Jones' total of 13. I want to win anyway, but after 14 months of trying for the record and failing, I am under even greater pressure. It's not likely that Bruce will birdie here, but if he does and I bogey, we're tied with four holes to play and he gets a big lift. I decide I must make at least a par somehow. The problem is that the pin is 215 yards away and I'm in tall grass with a large tree dead in my line. Hitting over the tree isn't an option: I can't get the ball up fast enough and still achieve the necessary distance. I could try to hook the ball around the tree to the right, but that's not my natural shot. Also, a hook requires a low angle of clubhead attack, which is very hard to achieve with good control from heavy grass. I decide to try to fade the ball around the tree.

THE SHOT: As always from rough, the ball will come out with reduced backspin and thus run more than normal. To allow for that, I go down a club to the 4-iron. I set up for a fade—body and clubface slightly open relative to the true target line—and address the ball a little back in my stance. Swinging back, I pick the club up sharply with my arms, reducing my body turn, then punch steeply down onto the back of the ball with a very firm left-hand grip to prevent the face turning over as the grass wraps around the hosel. The ball squirts out hot, fades perfectly around the tree, and runs up onto the green about 30 feet from the hole. I two-putt, Bruce bogeys, and half an hour later, a lifelong dream has finally come true.

THE LESSON: When a trouble situation permits bending the ball either way, always go with the shot shape that is most natural to you.

The 1974 PGA Championship
Tanglewood Park (West Course), Clemmons, N.C.

18th hole, par 4, 440 yards

HANG TOUGH

WITH THE RIGHT STRATEGY

THE SITUATION: Eighteenth tee, final round, one stroke back of Lee Trevino. An hour previously I'd gotten the feeling Lee had pretty much slammed the door on me, but by surprisingly three-putting the 17th, he has just opened it again. That gets my adrenaline really pumping, because I'm the defending champion and this is my last chance of the year to win a major.

MY THOUGHT PROCESS: The tee shot is a hard call. On the one hand the hole is playing long and anything more than birdie may not be good enough, which says, "Go for it with the driver to set up the shortest possible approach." On the other hand, to have a realistic chance at birdie I must hit the green in two, which would be impossible from the lush, six-inch Bermuda rough, which says, "Get it safely in the fairway." Finally, Lee makes the decision for me. I can tell the three-putt hasn't helped his nerves, and by getting my tee shot in the fairway

first, I believe I'll put even more pressure on him. Then, if I can put my ball on the green first, I'll keep it on, even if he also drives well.

THE SHOT: I pull out the 3-wood and, swinging well within myself, hit the ball about 250 yards into the heart of the fairway. Nervous or not, Trevino grabs his driver and nails it about 20 yards past me, also on the short grass. That puts him over the first hurdle, but I can still raise the second a few notches by getting my approach very close. Going with the 4-iron, I fail to do so, leaving the ball some 20 feet from the cup. Lee hits a 6-iron inside me, and, after my birdie attempt just misses, two-putts his way to the title.

THE LESSON: Don't let instinct override intelligence in last-gasp situations. My execution wasn't good enough on this occasion, but I believe my strategy was right on the nose. Figure out and play the percentages because they will definitely pay off over the long haul. And do so starting with your opening stroke on each hole, remembering that you are never going to win any trophies for macho tee shots.

**The 1975
Masters Tournament**
Augusta National Golf Club,
Augusta, Ga.

15th hole, par 5, 500 yards

CHOOSE A CLUB

THAT'S WORKED BEFORE

THE SITUATION: Final round. Tom Weiskopf, playing with Johnny Miller in the group immediately behind me, has been breathing down my neck all day. Now I'm standing in the center of the 15th fairway after a solid drive, figuring the distance to the pin. I've just bogeyed the 14th with a sloppy approach and three putts, which put Tom and me in a tie again. Miller is three strokes back of us. Caddie Willie Peterson agrees with me on the distance: 242 yards to the hole.

MY THOUGHT PROCESS: Both Weiskopf and Miller can reach the 15th green with irons if they hit good drives, so I have to assume they'll birdie or even eagle the hole. That means I can't play safe—I *must* birdie or better. Normally I'd favor the 3-wood for a shot of this distance, but going long here risks big trouble, including a possible water penalty if I draw it a fraction. Also, the 1-iron has been my favorite club all through my career, thus I'm far more confident with it than with the 3-wood. And the adrenaline is gushing. "OK, the 1-iron," I tell Willie.

THE SHOT: First-tee nerves had made my swing too short, producing a bad opening drive. As a consequence, I'd settled on "Complete the backswing" as the afternoon's key swing thought, and it had served me well. With that thought now up front and center again, I hit one of the three finest maximum-pressure 1-iron shots of my life. (The other two: my tee shot to the par-3 17th at Pebble Beach in the final round of the '72 Open and my approach to the last green during the final round of the '67 Open at Baltusrol.) Absolutely nailed dead on the stick, I thought for a moment the ball might actually go in the hole for a double eagle. It didn't, finishing about 20 feet from the hole. Nor did I make the eagle. But the birdie proved critical a little while later, when I ended up winning by a stroke over Tom and Johnny when both players missed birdie putts on the final hole.

THE LESSON: When in doubt between two clubs, go with the one that's served you best in the past—and the same with your selection of key swing images.

The 1975 Masters
Augusta (Ga.) National
Golf Club
16th hole, par 3,
170 yards

WHEN TO GO FOR BROKE

THE SITUATION: I'm on the 16th green 40 feet short and left of the hole after a slightly heavy 5-iron. My playing partner, Tom Watson, is on his way back to the tee to reload after finding his first tee shot in the lake. This gives me time to watch Tom Weiskopf and Johnny Miller back at the nearby 15th green. Both birdie. That puts Weiskopf one ahead of me and Miller one behind. Watson hits his second tee shot on the green, a little farther from the hole than mine, but on much the same line. Thus, Tom will putt first.

MY THOUGHT PROCESS: The pin is cut scarily near the front of the plateau in the back right corner of the green. I watch *very* carefully how Tom's ball rolls. As I expect, it begins to curve sharply to the left soon after cresting the hill. The confirmation is helpful, but the thought uppermost in my mind as I begin my own checking is, "Get close and make par." A three- or four-footer at this stage on a green this slick is a lot more golf than I care to think about.

THE SHOT: Examining the line from behind the ball, I'm still thinking, "Make par and go on your way." Then, straightening up after one last look, I realize I can "see" the line in my mind's eye about as clearly as I ever have on a putt of this length. As I complete my aim and setup, still with the picture of both line and speed sharp in my head, the thought becomes, *"Make it."* I strike the ball solidly and dead on the intended line. As it gets within about a dozen feet of the cup, I just know there's no way it can miss and I lift my putter high overhead. As the ball drops, both my caddie, Willie Peterson, and I turn into Indian war dancers. Half an hour later, I've won a record fifth Masters.

THE LESSON: Trust your senses whenever you're "seeing" putts well *and* stroking solidly. You aren't ever going to make a lot of 40-footers, but when both line and speed get into absolutely perfect mind's eye-focus, go ahead and go for broke.

DON'T FORCE A FLAWED SWING

THE SITUATION: I've won the Masters in April, and with three holes to play in the U.S. Open, the second leg of the modern Grand Slam seems well within reach. This has been one of those "giveaway" weeks when no one who has gained an advantage has been able to capitalize on it. I feel that if I can par in, I'll either win outright or make a playoff. The only trouble is that I am using what I call an artificial golf swing.

MY THOUGHT PROCESS: Try as I might in preparing for the championship, I am unable to find a way to get to my left side properly coming down. That makes fading the ball consistently—my standard shot—very difficult. Finally, I decide that my best chance lies in going with a right-to-left game. It's worked well enough to keep me in the race, but now, with the configuration of the hole just crying out for a fade from the tee, I'm compelled to try the correct shot. What I visualize is a high driver starting down the left edge of the fairway and sliding softly into its center.

THE SHOT: When you've ingrained one swing pattern and then suddenly change to another, particularly with the driver, and especially when you're in the pressure cooker, you're taking a pretty big gamble. This one fails. I set up perfectly for the fade, then involuntarily switch to a draw action starting down. Failing to clear my lower body out of the way fast enough, I close the clubface through the ball and pull-hook it deep into the woods. I make a bogey and follow it with two more at 17 and 18 for a 289 score. John Mahaffey and Lou Graham finish at 287, and Lou wins the playoff the next day.

THE LESSON: A good player, swinging at his peak and feeling confident, can work the ball either way at will. A good player, fighting a fault and not entirely sure of himself, is inviting trouble when he tries to get too much out of his game.

The 1975 U.S. Open
Medinah (Ill.) Country Club (No. 3)
16th hole, par 4, 452 yards

THE RIGHT TIME TO GAMBLE

THE SITUATION: Coming off No. 15 in the third round I'm five strokes ahead and the big cushion contributes to a piece of sloppiness. My caddie, Angelo Argea, hands me the driver and heads on down the fairway. When I get to the tee, I find the markers 30 yards forward of their regular position. That means I should hit a 3-wood for proper positioning of the lay-up second shot. For a moment I consider calling Angie back, but it's been a long, hot afternoon. I decide to hit an "easy" driver. The ball finishes in the water hazard way left. I drop out under penalty of one stroke, into a flyer lie, and whale a 6-iron 230 yards into the right rough smack behind a large tree.

MY THOUGHT PROCESS: The tree is about 30 feet high and only a few yards in front of me. The pin is 137 yards away. There is a pond immediately in front of the green. The ball, tree, pond and pin are all in line with one another. I'm lying three. I could chip the ball out sideways, then pitch to the green and two-putt. That would be a 7. I could go for the green, land in the water, then pitch on and two-putt. That would be 8. However, if I *make* the green and *one-putt* that would be a par 5. I have a handsome lead and there are 20 more holes to play after this one. I decide to go for it.

THE SHOT: Picking the club is a simple process of elimination: The pitching wedge won't give me enough distance and the 8-iron won't climb quickly enough, so it's a 9-iron. I open the face and set the ball well forward in my stance to insure fast height, tell myself, "Stay still," and swing as hard as I can. The ball clears the tree by a few inches and the pond by a few feet and stops 30 feet past the hole. I make the putt, finish with a 67 and cruise to a comfortable victory the next day.

THE LESSON: I looked this shot over *very* carefully and the more I did so the more confident I felt that I could make it. Also, I'd still be well in the hunt even if I failed. Such a combination is the time to gamble.

The 1975
PGA Championship,
Firestone Country Club
(South Course),
Akron, Ohio

16th hole, par 5, 625 yards

STAY STILL

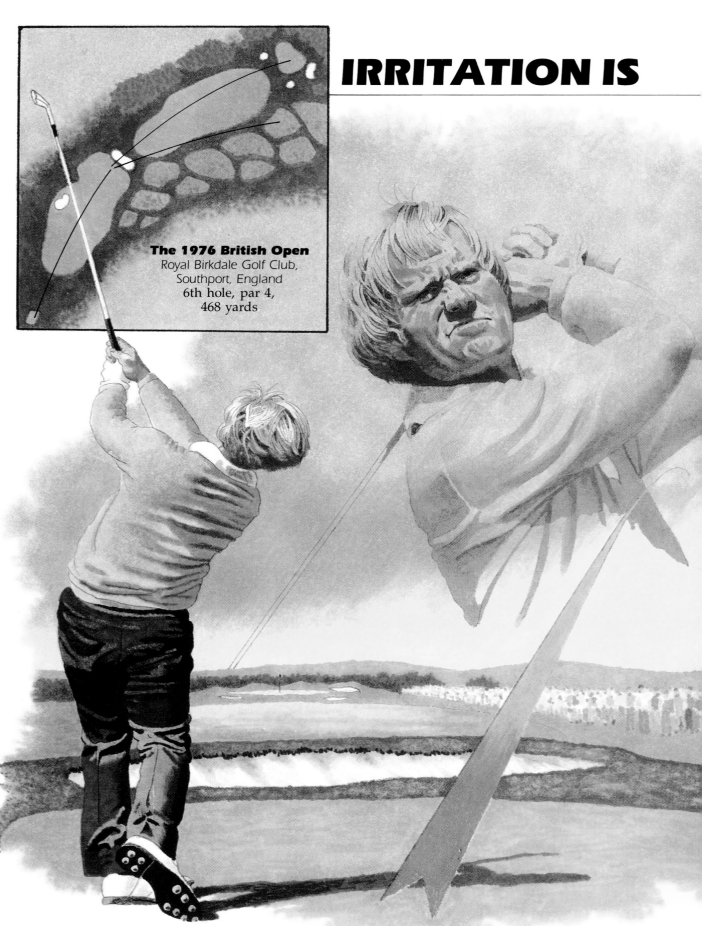

IRRITATION IS

The 1976 British Open
Royal Birkdale Golf Club,
Southport, England
6th hole, par 4,
468 yards

THE FATHER OF FAILURE

THE SITUATION: Starting the final round, I'm three shots back of Johnny Miller and five adrift of—until this championship—an unknown 19-year-old by the name of Severiano Ballesteros. That situation improves with birdies at Nos. 3 and 4, and now I'm standing in the fairway of Birkdale's trickiest hole facing into a strong wind off the ocean and thinking with some irritation about what to do next.

MY THOUGHT PROCESS: The irritation is caused by the fact that I've been forced to lay up off the tee with the 1-iron, short of a heavily bunkered ridge crossing the fairway at a distance that no one in the field can possibly carry into today's wind. I've never liked holes that don't offer a logical progression of shots and this is a supreme example of such poor design (it's since been improved somewhat). Even less do I like the options it has presented: to try to force a 1-iron some 235 yards through the wind to a small elevated green tightly situated between sandhills and dense willow scrub, or lay up with a lesser club and try to make par with a pitch and putt. Finally, I decide that if I'm going to have any chance of catching Seve and Johnny, I

just *have* to make par here, which translates into going for the green.

THE SHOT: As I pull out the 1-iron and start my aiming and setup procedure, I'm still conscious in the back of my mind that the hole today really is a par 5, and that if this wasn't the final round or I weren't so far back, there's no way I'd be attempting so high-risk a shot. I stay with my decision anyway and make an OK backswing. Then, trying to add that little extra oomph, I get ahead with my body coming down and push the ball dead right. It finishes so far out in the almost impenetrable willow scrub that I decide to not even go look for it, and so immediately drop another ball. A few minutes later, I've made 4 with it for 6 on the hole. A couple of hours later Johnny Miller is the champion.

THE LESSON: Thinking later about what happened, I decided the shot I'd attempted was comparable with trying to get the ball into the back left of the 17th green at St. Andrews when contending in the last round of an Open, which is something I'd never try to do. In other words, I stretched too hard mentally, which subconsciously triggered the physical failure.

WEIGH ALL THE POSSIBILITIES

THE SITUATION: Final round. After nine holes and playing well, I'm four strokes back of Tom Watson, who's in the group behind me. He's just put together four straight birdies on the fifth through the eighth holes. Tom has been "coming" fast since his first major win in the 1975 British Open, and it's obvious that he's now "here." Responding to the challenge, I birdie 10, 12, 13 and 15. As I walk to my ball on the left side of the 18th fairway, we're tied.

MY THOUGHT PROCESS: "Make par," I tell myself, "and you'll at least be in a playoff." As usual, the pin's tucked on the lower left of the green behind the bunker. I favor a solid 6-iron to the heart of the green, setting up a two-putt par. Just as I've finished planning and visualizing the shot, there's a big roar from the 17th green. Tom's birdied, to go ahead by one. I haven't "programmed" that possibility, and it shakes me. I back off and start refiguring. It's a whole new ball game. Now I *must birdie* to tie, assuming he finishes with a par.

THE SHOT: I'm not sure even a hard 7-iron will reach the green, but a solid 6 will almost certainly leave me beyond possible one-putt range. The process of elimination produces the strategy: a soft 6-iron. Normally that would be a cinch, and especially in a situation like this: The greater the challenge, the stronger my motivation and the sharper my reflexes. But this time I can't settle, can't reprogram thoroughly, can't dampen the adrenaline flow. I make a poor swing, catch the ball a hair fat, and know immediately it won't clear the bunker. I float it out of the sand to 12 feet, but the putt slips by for a bogey. A few minutes later, Watson pars the hole to win his first Masters by two strokes.

THE LESSON: Never take anything for granted at this game. By failing to consider the possibility of Tom birdieing, I opened myself to a psychological uppercut at a moment of extreme pressure, then couldn't recover from it.

**The 1977
Masters
Tournament**
Augusta National
Golf Club,
Augusta, Ga.

18th hole, par 4, 405 yards

The 1977 British Open Championship
Turnberry Golf Club
(Ailsa Course),
Turnberry, Scotland

17th hole, par 5,
515 yards

GO WITH YOUR

INSTINCTS ON CRITICAL PUTTS

THE SITUATION: Paired together, Tom Watson and I had each produced 65s in the third round to tie for the lead. Now, with two holes to play on the final afternoon, we're still all locked up after four hours of heavy punching and counterpunching, highlighted by a Watson slam-dunk from way off the green for a birdie at the par-3 15th. Both of us hit good drives on 17, then Tom nails a 3-iron about 25 feet from the hole. My solid 4-iron hangs right, leaving an extremely awkward little pitch from a fluffy lie. I feel I've done well when the ball stops 5½ feet from the hole.

MY THOUGHT PROCESS: Watson's a superb putter, so I accept that his birdie, if not an eagle, is a foregone conclusion. That means my putt is a must to avoid both a one-stroke deficit with one hole to play *plus* a big psychological lift for Tom. I've been putting well, and over the years have made an awful lot of pressure putts from about this distance. I feel I can drop this one.

THE SHOT: Tom's 25-footer is on pretty much my own line, and I watch his ball very carefully as he leaves it dead and then taps in. As it neared the hole, his putt broke slightly to the left. After a considerable amount of checking—this is no time to rush—I decide mine will do the same. I make a good backstroke and hit the ball solidly and exactly on the intended line. It stays straight and stays out. I birdie the final hole off a bad drive with a long putt for a 66, but Tom tops me with a three-foot birdie for a 65, and he's the champion.

THE LESSON: Be guided by what the other fellow's ball does on the greens when the lines are similar, but in the end go with what your own instincts tell you. What you can never precisely "read" is the force or speed someone else applies to a putt, and that is generally the most crucial factor.

THE BEAR GETS A

BAD BREAK, TOO

The 1977 PGA Championship
Pebble Beach Golf Links
Pebble Beach, Calif.

17th hole, par 3, 209 yards

THE SITUATION: Walking off the 10th green in the final round, I'm six shots behind Gene Littler. As I reach the 17th tee, we're tied. Gene's made five bogeys in six holes. For me, it's been one of those "can't make anything happen" days with one birdie, one bogey and 14 pars. But I can still reach out and grab a record-tying fifth PGA—and I want that badly after narrowly losing the Masters and British Open earlier in the season. Lanny Wadkins is now right in it with Littler, but chances are I'll at least tie them if I finish with two pars.

MY THOUGHT PROCESS: A birdie is always a possibility at Pebble Beach's par-5 18th, but I play golf best one stroke and one hole at a time, so I keep my mind in the here and now. Five years previously I almost holed a 1-iron at 17, which locked up the U.S. Open. Now, standing on the tee, I briefly relive that memory for added resolve. I'll take a birdie, of course, but my goal is par. To be sure of a par requires hitting the half of the figure-eight green containing the cup, in this case the left portion directly beyond the bunker.

THE SHOT: Few par 3s require more accurate club selection than this one, but the computer clicks out "3-iron" decisively and caddie Angelo Argea confirms it. In the 1972 Open I saved the 1-iron with a lucky downswing adjustment after starting back incorrectly. This time I make a perfect swing and, watching the ball in the air, am certain it will finish in birdie range. Instead, it catches the crown in the center of the figure eight, kicks sharply right and finally stops in the froghair 50 feet from the pin. There's no way to get the chip close, and I miss the resulting 15-footer. I also miss a tying birdie chance from twice that distance at 18. Lanny beats Gene on the third hole of the PGA's first sudden-death playoff.

THE LESSON: There will always be times in golf when you just have to live with the pain of a "bad break" and wait for the next time. Unlucky bounces are as intrinsic a part of the game as good ones, and in the long run they generally even out. Remember, it would be a heck of a dull game if the result of every shot were 100 percent predictable.

The 1978 British Open Championship
The Old Course
St. Andrews,
Scotland

17th hole, par 4, 461 yards

PLAY FOR YOUR

SCORE, NOT YOUR EGO

THE SITUATION: No major victories in almost three years and now I've just gone one ahead of playing partner Simon Owen with a birdie to his bogey at 16. The Road Hole 17th is playing downwind for the first time all week. I resist the temptation to go with the driver and hit a 3-wood dead over my aiming spot and safely in the fairway. Simon's driven beautifully with the big stick all day, but now he turns one too much into the left rough, then finds the road with his second shot.

MY THOUGHT PROCESS: Although it's unlikely, Simon could still scramble for a par, and the 18th offers him a strong birdie possibility. Also, Peter Oosterhuis, behind us, isn't out of it. So the next shot could be the ball game for me. Somehow, I've got to make a 4. But how? To get all the way back to the hole squeezed between the pot bunker and the road, would require perfect clubbing, perfect execu-

tion and perfect luck on the bounce. Miss just one fraction into either hazard and I'm fighting for a 5, maybe more.

THE SHOT: First, the target. There's an ample-sized hollow fronting the green mown tight enough to putt from. Hitting into it leaves a long and difficult roll, but there is no way I'll make more than 5 from there. OK, now the club. Enough to swing easily, but not enough to reach the road or bunker even if caught extra-solidly. It computes to the 6-iron. I hit it perfectly, followed by maybe the best 60-foot putt I've ever struck that didn't actually drop. Fifteen minutes later I've won my third British Open.

THE LESSON: Never be a hero when you don't have to be. Look for the highest percentage or least pressured shot after a cool analysis of the situation. Play for the scorecard, not for your ego.

The 1979 Masters
Augusta (Ga.) National Golf Club
17th hole, par 4,
400 yards

BELIEVE IN YOUR

SWING UNDER PRESSURE

THE SITUATION: I tee off in the last round almost an hour ahead of the leaders. I'm eight shots off the pace and figure I'll need no worse than 67 to get anyone's attention. I turn the front nine in one under par, then birdie 10 and 13, make par from the water at 15 and birdie 16. One more birdie and I'll have my 67. A glance at the leader board indicates that it might just be good enough. No one seems to be doing much behind me. Eighteen is no birdie hole, so it had better be now at 17. I hit an excellent drive, but the ball finishes in a grassy lie.

MY THOUGHT PROCESS: The 17th at Augusta may not look too hard from outside the ropes, but the second shot is always tricky. You have to carry the front bunkers, but then stop the ball fast on a hard green that falls off at the back and both sides. I have 147 yards to the hole and 135 yards to carry the front bunker. I'm tempted to hit the 9-iron, but then check myself with the thought that if I don't catch the ball perfectly I could be in sand. I decide the best shot is an easy 8-iron, straight for the flag.

THE SHOT: Swinging easy is a guaranteed way to swing well. I flush the ball and fear immediately that it's too much, even without the flyer effect—the reduced backspin—of the grassy lie. I'm right. I can't see the ball land, but there's a big gallery groan. When I get up there, I'm ready to groan, too. The ball is way down the bank behind the green. I fail to get it up and down, then par the 18th for a 69. An hour later, the bogey at 17 has cost me a place in a playoff, won by Fuzzy Zoeller from Tom Watson and Ed Sneed.

THE LESSON: I hit the wrong club because I let myself get negative about what would happen if I failed to hit the correct one perfectly. It was a classic example of a very common golfing fault at all levels of the game: not trusting your swing and not being aggressive under pressure. Once you think you've determined the proper play, always go for it without second-guessing yourself.

**The 1980
U. S. Open
Championship**
Baltusrol Golf Club,
Springfield, N.J.
17th hole, par 5, 630 yards

GO WITH YOUR

THE SITUATION: Final round, the 630-yard par-5 17th. After a good drive and 2-iron, I'm 88 yards from the pin, which is set front and left. Miss the green left and it's big trouble. I'm two strokes ahead of Isao Aoki, who now hits his third shot five feet from the pin. I've played with Isao all four rounds and, the way he's putted, I just *know* he'll make this one. The final hole is another par 5, and I figure he'll birdie that, too.

MY THOUGHT PROCESS: I'm sure I need at least a birdie and a par on the last two holes to avoid a playoff, and I'm feeling exceptional pressure. I've revamped my entire game, worked my tail off all season, but haven't won in almost two years. As well as I've played this week, it's been hard not to wonder whether the wheels will stay on—and pitching has never been my strongest suit. When you're uptight like this, there's a strong urge to relieve the tension by rushing. I force myself to think this shot through very deliberately. Finally I decide to play to the right of the pin, both to protect against the trouble to the left and to leave myself an uphill putt. But which club? I can hit the ball 88 yards with either a three-quarter pitching wedge or a full sand wedge.

THE SHOT: The faster the adrenaline flows, the tougher "part"-shots become. Pumped up, you tend to take too long a backswing, then either hit the ball way strong or involuntarily slow down through impact and leave it short or drag it off line, or both. Thus you're far better off with a club you can swing fully and freely, and that's why I choose the sand wedge in this case. I hit the ball pin-high 23 feet to the right of the cup, and when I make the putt suddenly all the tension evaporates. I'm able to play the final hole conservatively, luck out with another good putt for a final birdie, win my fourth U.S. Open, break my own 72-hole scoring record and enjoy one of the happiest evenings of my life.

SHOT

THE LESSON: The greater the pressure, the less you should try to "finesse" the shot. Take your time in analyzing the situation, then go with the highest-percentage club—the one you can swing most normally.

The 1980 U.S. Open
Baltusrol Golf Club,
Springfield, N.J.

18th hole,
par 5, 542 yards

KEEP THE FAITH

AND DON'T CHICKEN OUT

THE SITUATION: Round two, final hole. Caught exceptionally solidly, my second shot finishes through the green under a television camera. I get a free drop clear, but the ball comes to rest on baked, sparsely grassed ground where people have been walking for days, a really unpleasant lie. The pin is tucked tight in the back left corner of the green which is fast and sloping away from me. And there's a sizable, rough-covered hump between me and the putting surface.

MY THOUGHT PROCESS: After a 63 in the opening round, I've fumbled enough on the back nine today to let a lot of good players close in. Getting up and down here for birdie would help that situation a little and my spirits a lot. But how? I have no chance of maneuvering the ball within one-putt range with my old pitching technique. A new method I've recently learned from Phil Rodgers ought to do it, but here is a situation leaving absolutely no margin for error. If I don't make 4, I am almost certain to make 6, or more. I decide now is the time to find out how much pressure the combination of new method and old nerves can sustain.

THE SHOT: The technique Phil taught me involves setting the weight left while inclining the upper body and head to the right, then using exceptionally light grip pressure and a great deal of wrist action to slip the wide-open clubface of the sand wedge gently beneath the ball and loft it almost straight up so that it lands very softly and stops almost immediately. As always on any finesse shot, I carefully rehearse the action with plenty of practice swings while visualizing how I want the ball to behave. When the lie is as bad as this one, there's a great risk of flinching on the downswing. As I get set over the ball, I remind myself to go through physically with what I've committed to mentally. The swing feels textbook smooth, and the shot comes off exactly as I've planned. As the ball stops tap-in distance from the cup, Bob Rosburg, doing TV commentary nearby, shakes his head and says, "People don't know just how good a shot that was." I give him a grin and a wink and say, "No, but *I* do."

THE LESSON: Once you believe you have finally learned how to do something with a golf club, have faith in yourself and go ahead and do it whenever the situation requires. In other words, don't chicken out. That's the only way to get better at this game.

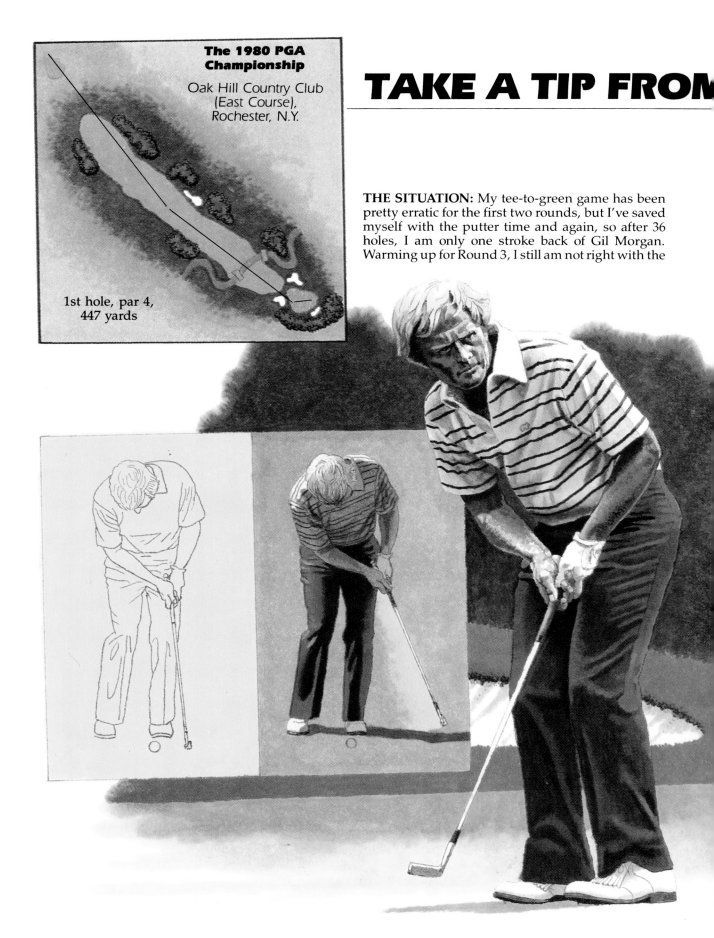

The 1980 PGA Championship

Oak Hill Country Club (East Course), Rochester, N.Y.

1st hole, par 4, 447 yards

TAKE A TIP FROM

THE SITUATION: My tee-to-green game has been pretty erratic for the first two rounds, but I've saved myself with the putter time and again, so after 36 holes, I am only one stroke back of Gil Morgan. Warming up for Round 3, I still am not right with the

SOMEONE WHO KNOWS YOU

big shots, which adds to my nervousness on the opening hole. I hit an OK drive, then a mediocre approach that stops on the front right of the green at least 50 feet from the cup, which is cut back left. Already I'm putting pressure on my putting again, and I can't help wondering how long it will hold up.

MY THOUGHT PROCESS: My putting had gradually deteriorated after winning the U.S. Open in June, and I had gotten more and more gloomy about it right up until the week before the PGA. Then, as we were playing a round at Muirfield Village, my son Jackie said that he thought he'd spotted the problem: I was stopping my hands and the putterhead at the ball, or breaking off the stroke too soon. Jackie showed me what he meant, and how it caused the clubhead to move left of the target through the ball, preventing a solid hit and pulling a lot of putts off line. He'd also suggested an antidote, and now, as I finish figuring line and speed on this opening 50-footer, I key on it as hard as I know how.

THE SHOT: Jackie's suggested cure was to concentrate on swinging my hands—and therefore the putterhead—firmly *through* rather than *to* the ball, and then on out toward the target for what at first seemed like an exaggerated distance. This helped almost immediately, and so we had worked hard for the next few days on breaking the old habit and getting me comfortable with the new feel. It had held up beautifully both in practice and over the first two rounds at Oak Hill, but, with the pressure my in-and-out long game was applying, I couldn't help but wonder whether it would go the distance. Over the ball, I reminded myself, "Straight through to the target" one more time, then stroked. The impact felt great, the line looked better and better as the ball reached the cup, and when it fell in, all my doubts instantly vanished. The following evening, still putting like crazy, I'd won my fifth PGA by seven strokes.

THE LESSON: When you're struggling and someone who really knows your game offers a suggestion, listen up hard.

PRACTICE YOUR PATIENCE,

THE SITUATION: Leading by four shots at the halfway mark with 70-65—135, I make a good start in the third round, then get a little sloppy to turn in 37. That allows Tom Watson, playing immediately ahead and out in 34, to pull within a single stroke as I reach the 12th tee. The pin is tucked behind the bunker in the far right portion of the green. As I'm setting up to the ball, there's an enormous roar from the crowd watching Tom at 13. I have to assume he's hit his second shot very close, perhaps even—from all the uproar—within tap-in eagle range.

MY THOUGHT PROCESS: Rule No. 1 of major championship golf is never to hit the ball to the right of the front bunker at No. 12 at Augusta National, and that certainly isn't my game plan prior to the hullabaloo for Tom's shot. Also, you don't suddenly dump your game plan because of a single move by another player. Nevertheless, even though perhaps more subconsciously than consciously, I change mine. I'm playing well, my swing feels super . . . . Maybe, just maybe, I can get away with it one time . . . can just squeeze it in there . . . .

THE SHOT: I am certain the 6-iron is the correct club. I make a very good pass and a solid strike with it, but sense as soon as my eyes pick up the ball in flight that I may have big trouble. A moment later that's confirmed. Just a few feet to the right of being perfect, but a fatal few feet, the ball lands on the front fringe of the green, spins smartly backward, then rolls slowly down the shaved bank into Rae's Creek. I eventually walk off with a double bogey, then follow it with a bogey at 13 after again trying for too much and finding the creek to the right of that green. The following evening, Tom Watson wins his second Masters. Johnny Miller and I are tied for second, two strokes back.

THE LESSON: If I had stuck to my game plan regarding my target area, the ball would have cleared the bunker and finished on the green left of the pin within easy two-putt and possible one-putt range. Instead, I became impatient, which boils down to a lack of discipline, then did it again on the next hole. That is an absolutely guaranteed way to lose golf tournaments.

TOO

ERASE THE TAPE AFTER A BAD

The 1982 U.S. Open
Pebble Beach Golf Links,
Pebble Beach, Calif.
8th hole, par 4, 431 yards

BREAK YOU DIDN'T MAKE

THE SITUATION: Three strokes behind Tom Watson and Bill Rogers starting the last round, I open with a bogey, follow with a par at the very birdieable par-5 second, and am seemingly out of the hunt. But standing in the eighth fairway, I'm co-leader with Rogers after five consecutive birdies, including a near hole-in-one at the par-3 fifth and an exciting 1-iron to the green out of a very tight lie at the par-5 sixth. I'm also in ideal position after a 3-wood tee shot.

MY THOUGHT PROCESS: The upcoming approach is my favorite shot in golf, and the birdie string makes me even more "up" about it than usual. The wind is blowing slightly from left to right, or partially helping, and the hole is cut in the center right section of the green. I figure the yardages and wind factor a couple of times, and each time the answer is: solid 6-iron just left of the flag. That way, even if the ball draws or fades slightly, I should be putting.

THE SHOT: I make what feels like an excellent swing, and the ball starts out exactly where I've aimed it. Watching it, I begin to think about birdie No. 6. Then, suddenly, the ball starts to drift, until finally toward the end of its flight, I'm telling it to "Get in the sand!" The reason is the almost foot-high collar of lush, matted rough around many of the bunkers this year, mandated by the USGA and gloatingly referred to by its Open committee members as "character." I've rarely seen a dumber set-up on a golf course, and I've hated it all week, and now, finally, it has got me—but good. Just inches off in my ball flighting, and ending up in the collar only 15 feet from the cup, I have difficulty finding the ball. When I do, I have absolutely no chance of getting it close. I hack out to seven or so feet, miss the putt, and subconsciously let my irritation take something off my momentum. A couple of hours later, following his famous holed pitch shot at the 17th, Tom Watson wins his first U.S. Open.

THE LESSON: The hardest thing in golf is to stay in overdrive after a really bad break off an almost perfect shot. I thought at the time I'd done a pretty good job, but later I came to realize just how much I'd give to play those last 10 holes over.

IT'S NOT OVER

The 1983 PGA Championship
Riviera Country Club,
Pacific Palisades, Calif.
18th hole, par 4,
447 yards

UNTIL THE WINNING SHOT

THE SITUATION: First round, No. 18, one of golf's truly great finishing holes. Even though it's blind, I've always loved the tee shot for the way it sets you up and tells you where to hit. This time I've nailed the driver but the ball has ended up a little more to the right side of the fairway than I'd like. My putter has been cool all day and I'm at even par. There are a lot of guys under par, and a few of them a long way under.

MY THOUGHT PROCESS: I'd played some good golf the previous week to finish third in the Canadian Open, and feel as though I'm swinging even better now than then. Consequently, I'm pretty up about my chances, and know I'll be even higher if I can close with a birdie. If I could go straight for the pin, 7-iron would be plenty of club, but I need a touch of fade to get around the big eucalyptus tree that juts out into the fairway. I decide on a smooth 6-iron.

THE SHOT: I've always controlled the amount I fade the ball by how much at address I align my shoulders, hips and feet left of the direct target line, along with the degree to which I open the clubface. Now I get the clubface alignment right but don't open my body sufficiently, which means the ball doesn't start far enough left. It catches the one skinny little branch sticking out all by itself, and a few minutes later I'm walking off the green with a double-bogey 6 for a two-over-par 73. The weak finish inspires friend Jim Murray to write a fine obituary of me in the *Los Angeles Times* the following morning, which in turn inspires me to a neat 65. I add a 71 in the third round, then finish with a 66 to lose to Hal Sutton by a single stroke.

THE LESSON: I was eight off the lead after the first round, seven after the second, and six after the third, but I managed to remain patient and keep playing my game and suddenly, coming down the stretch, I had a chance to win. I can't think of a finer example of what I believe to be the most important lesson of all about golf: the game is never over until the shot that beats you has actually been executed.

The 1986 Masters
Augusta (Ga.) National Golf Club
Eighth hole, par 5, 535 yards

IT WAS A LUCKY

BREAK THAT GOT ME GOING

THE SITUATION: My tee-to-green game has improved more and more the first three days of the tournament, so, starting the last round four strokes behind Greg Norman, I figure I'm still in it if I can only make a few putts. I drop a curly one on No. 2 for a birdie, but then three-putt the fourth and miss a tiddler for birdie at the sixth. Standing on the eighth tee, I'm even par for the round and making no impression on anyone, particularly myself. I decide to go for a tee shot that will let me reach the green in two shots. The ball is hit far, but pushed into the pine trees to the right.

MY THOUGHT PROCESS: About 20 feet ahead of me there is a six-foot-wide opening between a couple of big pine trees, through which I could safely punch an iron within easy pitching distance of the green. With any kind of a lead that's what I would do, with no hesitation. But I have to get moving if I'm going to give myself a chance. My yardages tell me I'm 3-wood distance from the green. Looking at the gap, I figure if I can keep the ball down and put a little cut on it while still hitting it solidly, I might just get home.

THE SHOT: You have to get a lot of things exactly right to pull off a shot like this, most notably at address the proper mix of open body and clubface alignment to impart a precise amount of cut-spin to the ball, combined with the proper positioning in relation to your feet to keep it low. I slip slightly somewhere with that formula, and push the shot a little. To the right of the right-hand tree is another fat pine, with a gap of no more than 12 inches between the two trees. The ball whistles cleanly through that little hole and finishes just right of the green, from where I pitch to about 10 feet and two-putt for par.

THE LESSON: If my ball had caught one of those trees, I might still be there. But sometimes when *winning* rather than placing high is what it's all about, you just have to take chances. There always has been and always will be a lot of luck in golf, and this time it worked in my favor.

IF HE'S GOOD,

The 1986 Masters Tournament
Augusta (Ga.) National Golf Club,
9th hole, par 4,
435 yards

USE YOUR CADDIE'S EYES

THE SITUATION: Despite a lucky break with my second shot at No. 8, I still only par the hole. That keeps me even par for the day and only two under for the tournament, which is still way off the pace. Walking down the ninth fairway after a big drive, I tell my eldest son, who is caddieing for me, "Jack, I sure would love to birdie here, because without that I figure the best I can hope for is 67, which may not be quite good enough." I then hit my second shot with the pitching wedge about 12 feet to the right of and behind the hole.

MY THOUGHT PROCESS: This is a very slick green, and I'm going both downhill and sidehill on it, so we both do a lot of looking. As I'm finally up behind the ball, figuring that it will break about five inches to the left, Jackie says to me, "Dad, I think it's going to go slightly left to right." That starts me rereading and rethinking the putt all over again, and suddenly I find what Jackie is seeing. The putt does not break as much to the left as I originally figured.

THE SHOT: Vagueness about line almost guarantees poor putting in that it produces sloppy blade alignment at address, a sense of which then prevents a positive, fully committed stroke. I aim and set up very carefully for the ball to break two inches from right to left. Confident about what I'm trying to do, I make a good, smooth stroke and find I've gotten both line and weight exactly right as the ball topples gently into the center of the cup.

THE LESSON: If you're in doubt, and have a caddie who can supply an informed second opinion, take full advantage of it. My sons know golf, and my game particularly, and they also have great eyes, so I always listen when they think they have something to contribute. But, most of all, never play a stroke with doubt in your mind. Make your decision, then be positive with the putt.

THEN IT WAS ADVERSITY THAT

THE SITUATION: I have just birdied the ninth, 10th and 11th with putts of 12, 25 and 20 feet, which gets me to three under par for the day and five under for the tournament. Behind me, Seve Ballesteros and Greg Norman are tied for the lead at seven under. I am now obviously very much in contention as I stand on the tee of Augusta National's most dangerous hole—maybe the scariest short par 3 any place on earth.

MY THOUGHT PROCESS: The flagstick is in its customary final-round position, tucked way right. From tee markers to cup is 162 yards, and it occurs to me I would need the 6-iron if I went directly at the pin. This thought reinforces my resolve *not* to go for it, with the high risk of water short and sand long, but rather to aim for the safer central area of the green beyond the single front bunker. The slight breeze seems to be from right to left and maybe even a touch against. I figure it's the 7-iron on the nose.

THE SHOT: However confident you are in your game and your club selection, the disaster potential of holes like this makes it hard to swing 100 percent freely. Over-guarding against going to the right, I pull the ball slightly and it finishes left and on the back fringe. From there, I play what I feel at impact is a super little pitch, but get an unlucky bounce that leaves me with a seven-foot putt for par, which I miss after it catches a spike mark a few inches ahead of the ball. After three birdies in a row, I've bogeyed the shortest hole on the course.

THE LESSON: At the 13th a few moments later I planned and hit my most attacking tee shot of the tournament, a hard, drawn 3-wood that came closer to the trees and creek than I'd have liked, but that set up an easy two-putt birdie and got me right back on the roll again. Without the adversity at No. 12 to knock the euphoria of the three consecutive birdies out of me, I might not have played as aggressively as I did over those closing holes, and in that regard it was a blessing in disguise.

SPURRED ME ON

The 1986 Masters
Augusta (Ga.) National Golf Club
12th hole, par 3, 155 yards

The 1986 Masters
Augusta (Ga.) National Golf Club
17th hole, par 4, 400 yards

I REMEMBERED

THE SHOT'S SECOND HALF

THE SITUATION: I've played the previous eight holes birdie-birdie-birdie-bogey-birdie-par-eagle-birdie. I figure one more birdie and I am definitely in with a chance to win. I plan to draw the drive to the left side of the fairway to give me the best angle to the pin, which is in the back right of the green. Coming down I'm a little slow with the lower body and turn the ball more than I want. It finishes well left in a tight lie on hard ground between a couple of pine trees.

MY THOUGHT PROCESS: The first thing I do, as always, is figure my yardage. It's 120 yards, which calls for the 9-iron. But, because of an overhanging limb, I must keep the ball low while also spinning it sufficiently to stop it quickly on one of Augusta National's firmest greens. The pitching wedge offers more spin, but also more height, which increases my risk of catching the limb. Finally, I decide it has to be the pitching wedge, kept low and hit with cut-spin.

THE SHOT: The more you cut a ball—spin it from left to right—the faster it stops but the higher it flies. To bring down the height, I position the ball about two inches farther back in my stance than normal. To be sure of imparting cut-spin, and to help promote a clean "nipping" of the ball from the close lie, I set my left hand on the club very firmly and keep it that way throughout the swing. The ball flies under the limb by about 18 inches, hits the green seemingly very hot, but immediately begins to check up because of the heavy spin. It finally stops 11 feet to the left of and slightly below the cup. When the putt drops I'm in the lead alone for the first time, and an hour later have won my sixth Masters and 20th major championship.

THE LESSON: Assess what the ball must do when it lands as well as while it is in the air, then use your imagination and inventive powers to try to come up with a shot that achieves *both* goals.

Jack Nicklaus'
Record
in Golf's
Major Championships

Jim McQueen

UNITED STATES AMATEUR CHAMPIONSHIP

1955—Country Club of Virginia, Richmond, Va.
Winner: E. Harvie Ward Jr. beat William Hyndman III 9 & 8
Nicklaus: Lost in first round to Robert W. Gardner 1 down

1956—Knollwood Club, Lake Forest, Ill.
Winner: E. Harvie Ward Jr. beat Charles Kocsis 5 & 4
Nicklaus: Lost in third round to Ronald E. Wenzler 3 & 2

1957—The Country Club, Brookline, Mass.
Winner: Hillman Robbins Jr. beat Dr. Frank M. Taylor Jr. 5 & 4
Nicklaus: Lost in fourth round to Richard L. Yost 3 & 2

1958—Olympic Country Club, San Francisco, Calif.
Winner: Charles R. Coe beat Thomas D. Aaron 5 & 4
Nicklaus: Lost in second round to E. Harvie Ward Jr. 1 down.

1959—Broadmoor Golf Club, Colorado Springs, Colo.
Winner: Nicklaus beat Charles R. Coe 1 up

1960—St. Louis Country Club, Clayton, Mo.
Winner: Deane R. Beman beat Robert W. Gardner 6 & 4
Nicklaus: Lost in fourth round to Charles F. Lewis 5 & 3

1961—Pebble Beach Golf Links, Monterey, Calif.
Winner: Nicklaus beat H. Dudley Wysong Jr. 8 & 6

BRITISH AMATEUR CHAMPIONSHIP

1959—Royal St. George's Golf Club, Sandwich, England
Winner: Deane R. Beman beat William Hyndman III 3 & 2
Nicklaus: Lost in quarterfinals to William Hyndman III 4 & 3

THE MASTERS TOURNAMENT

Augusta National Golf Club, Augusta, Ga.
1959 Winner: Art Wall Jr.—73-74-71-66—284
   *Nicklaus: 76-74—150. Missed cut.
1960 Winner: Arnold Palmer—67-73-72-70—282
   *Nicklaus: 75-71-72-75—293. T13th. T Low
amateur.
1961 Winner: Gary Player—69-68-69-74—280
   *Nicklaus: 70-75-70-72—287. T7th. Low
amateur.
1962 Winner: Arnold Palmer—70-66-69-75—280
(Defeated Gary Player and Dow Finsterwald in
playoff 68-71-77)
   Nicklaus: 74-75-70-72—291. T15th.
1963 Winner: Nicklaus—74-66-74-72—286
1964 Winner: Arnold Palmer—69-68-69-70—276
   Nicklaus: 71-73-71-67—282. T2nd.
1965 Winner: Nicklaus—67-71-64-69—271
1966 Winner: Nicklaus—68-76-72-72—288
(defeated Tommy Jacobs and Gay Brewer in
playoff 70-72-78).
1967 Winner: Gay Brewer—73-68-72-67—280
   Nicklaus: 72-79—151. Missed cut.
1968 Winner: Bob Goalby—70-70-71-66—277
   Nicklaus: 69-71-74-67—281. T5th.
1969 Winner: George Archer—67-73-69-72—281
   Nicklaus: 68-75-72-76—291. T24th.
1970 Winner: Billy Casper—72-68-68-71—279
(defeated Gene Littler in playoff 69-74)
   Nicklaus: 71-75-69-69—284. 8th.
1971 Winner: Charles Coody—66-73-70-70—279
   Nicklaus: 70-71-68-72—281. T2nd.
1972 Winner: Nicklaus—68-71-73-74—286
1973 Winner: Tommy Aaron—68-73-74-68—283
   Nicklaus: 69-77-73-66—285. T3rd.

1974 Winner: Gary Player—71-71-66-70—278
   Nicklaus: 69-71-72-69—281. T4th.
1975 Winner: Nicklaus—68-67-73-68—276
1976 Winner: Raymond Floyd—65-66-70-70—271
   Nicklaus: 67-69-73-73—282. T3rd.
1977 Winner: Tom Watson—70-69-70-67—276
   Nicklaus: 72-70-70-66—278. 2nd.
1978 Winner: Gary Player—72-72-69-64—277
   Nicklaus: 72-73-69-67—281. 7th.
1979 Winner: Fuzzy Zoeller—70-71-69-70—280
(defeated Ed Sneed and Tom Watson on 2nd hole
of sudden-death playoff)
   Nicklaus: 69-71-72-69—281. 4th.
1980 Seve Ballesteros—66-69-68-72—275
   Nicklaus: 74-71-73-73—291. T33rd.
1981 Winner: Tom Watson—71-68-70-71—280
   Nicklaus: 70-65-75-72—282. T2nd.
1982 Winner: Craig Stadler—75-69-67-73—284
(defeated Dan Pohl on 1st hole of sudden-death
playoff)
   Nicklaus: 69-77-71-75—292. T15th.
1983 Winner: Seve Ballesteros—68-70-73-69—280
   Nicklaus: 73-Withdrew
1984 Winner: Ben Crenshaw—67-72-70-68—277
   Nicklaus: 73-73-70-70—286. T18th.
1985 Winner: Bernhard Langer—72-74-68-68—282
   Nicklaus: 71-74-72-69—286. T6th.
1986 Winner: Nicklaus—74-71-69-65—279
1987 Winner: Larry Mize—70-72-72-71—285
(defeated Greg Norman and Seve Ballesteros on
2nd hole of sudden-death playoff)
   Nicklaus: 74-72-73-70—289. T7th.

*—Played as an amateur

UNITED STATES OPEN CHAMPIONSHIP

1957—Inverness Club, Toledo, Ohio
Winner: Dick Mayer—70-68-74-70—282
(defeated Cary Middlecoff in playoff 72-79)
*Nicklaus: 80-80—160. Missed cut.
1958—Southern Hills Country Club, Tulsa, Okla.
Winner: Tommy Bolt—71-71-69-72—283
*Nicklaus: 79-75-73-77—304. Tied 41st.
1959—Winged Foot Golf Club, Mamaroneck, N.Y.
Winner: Bill Casper—71-68-69-74—282
*Nicklaus: 77-77—154. Missed cut.
1960—Cherry Hills Country Club, Englewood, Colo.
Winner: Arnold Palmer—72-71-72-65—280
*Nicklaus: 71-71-69-71—282. 2nd.
1961—Oakland Hills Country Club, Birmingham, Mich.
Winner: Gene Littler—73-68-72-68—281
*Nicklaus: 75-69-70-70—284. T4th.
1962—Oakmont Country Club, Oakmont, Pa.
Winner: Nicklaus—72-70-72-69—283
(defeated Arnold Palmer in playoff 71-74)
1963—The Country Club, Brookline, Mass.
Winner: Julius Boros—71-74-76-72—293
(defeated Jacky Cupit and Arnold Palmer in playoff 70-73-76)
Nicklaus: 76-77—153. Missed cut.

1964—Congressional Country Club, Washington, D.C.
Winner: Ken Venturi—72-70-66-70—278
Nicklaus: 72-73-77-73—295. T23rd.
1965—Bellerive Country Club, Creve Coeur, Mo.
Winner: Gary Player—70-70-71-71—282
(defeated Kel Nagle in playoff 71-74)
Nicklaus: 78-72-73-76—299. T32nd.
1966—The Olympic Club, San Francisco, Calif.
Winner: Bill Casper—69-68-73-68—278
(defeated Arnold Palmer in playoff 69-73)
Nicklaus: 71-71-69-74—285. 3rd.
1967—Baltusrol Golf Club, Springfield, N.J.
Winner: Nicklaus—71-67-72-65—275
1968—Oak Hill Country Club, Rochester, N.Y.
Winner: Lee Trevino—69-68-69-69—275
Nicklaus: 72-70-70-67—279. 2nd.
1969—Champions Golf Club, Houston, Texas
Winner: Orville Moody—71-70-68-72—281
Nicklaus: 74-67-75-73—289. T25th.
1970—Hazeltine National Golf Club, Chaska, Minn.
Winner: Tony Jacklin—71-70-70-70—281
Nicklaus: 81-72-75-76—304. T51st.
1971—Merion Golf Club, Ardmore, Pa.
Winner: Lee Trevino—70-72-69-69—280
(defeated Nicklaus in playoff 68-71)
Nicklaus: 69-72-68-71—280. 2nd.

1972—Pebble Beach Golf Links, Pebble Beach, Calif.
Winner: Nicklaus—71-73-72-74—290
1973—Oakmont Country Club, Oakmont, Pa.
Winner: Johnny Miller—71-69-76-63—279
Nicklaus: 71-69-74-68—282. T4th.
1974—Winged Foot Golf Club, Mamaroneck, N.Y.
Winner: Hale Irwin—73-70-71-73—287
Nicklaus: 75-74-76-69—294. T10th.
1975—Medinah Country Club, Medinah, Ill.
Winner: Lou Graham—74-72-68-73—287
(defeated John Mahaffey in playoff 71-73)
Nicklaus: 72-70-75-72—289. T7th.
1976—Atlanta Athletic Club, Atlanta, Ga.
Winner: Jerry Pate—71-69-69-68—277
Nicklaus: 74-70-75-68—287. T11th.
1977—Southern Hills Country Club, Tulsa, Okla.
Winner: Hubert Green—69-67-72-70—278
Nicklaus: 74-68-71-72—285. T10th.
1978—Cherry Hills Country Club, Englewood, Colo.
Winner: Andy North—70-70-71-74—285
Nicklaus: 73-69-74-73—289. T6th.
1979—Inverness Club, Toledo, Ohio
Winner: Hale Irwin—74-68-67-75—284
Nicklaus: 74-77-72-68—291. T9th.
1980—Baltusrol Golf Club, Springfield, N.J.
Winner: Nicklaus—63-71-70-68—272
1981—Merion Golf Club, Ardmore, Pa.
Winner: David Graham—68-68-70-67—273
Nicklaus: 69-68-71-72—280. T6th.
1982—Pebble Beach Golf Links, Pebble Beach, Calif.
Winner: Tom Watson—72-72-68-70—282
Nicklaus: 74-70-71-69—284. 2nd.
1983—Oakmont Country Club, Oakmont, Pa.
Winner: Larry Nelson—75-73-65-67—280
Nicklaus: 73-74-77-76—300. T43rd.
1984—Winged Foot Golf Club, Mamaroneck, N.Y.
Winner: Fuzzy Zoeller—71-66-69-70—276
Nicklaus: 71-71-70-77—289. T21st.
1985—Oakland Hills Country Club, Birmingham, Mich.
Winner: Andy North—70-65-70-74—279
Nicklaus: 76-73—149. Missed cut.
1986—Shinnecock Hills Golf Club, Southampton, N.Y.
Winner: Raymond Floyd—75-68-70-66—279
Nicklaus: 77-72-67-68—284. T8th.
1987—Olympic Club, San Francisco, Calif.
Winner: Scott Simpson—71-68-70-68—277
Nicklaus: 70-68-76-77—291. T46th.

*—Played as an amateur

BRITISH OPEN CHAMPIONSHIP

1962—Royal Troon Golf Club, Troon, Scotland
Winner: Arnold Palmer—71-69-67-69—276
Nicklaus: 80-72-74-79—305. T34th.

1963—Royal Lytham & St. Annes Golf Club, Lytham St. Annes, England
Winner: Bob Charles—68-72-66-71—277
(defeated Phil Rodgers in playoff 69-71—140, 72-76—148
Nicklaus: 71-67-70-70—278. 3rd.

1964—The Old Course, St. Andrews, Scotland
Winner: Tony Lema—73-68-68-70—279
Nicklaus: 76-74-66-68—284. 2nd.

1965—Royal Birkdale Golf Club, Southport, England
Winner: Peter Thomson—74-68-72-71—285
Nicklaus: 73-71-77-73—294. T12th.

1966—The Honourable Company of Edinburgh Golfers, Muirfield, Scotland
Winner: Nicklaus—70-67-75-70—282

1967—Royal Liverpool Golf Club, Hoylake, England
Winner: Roberto De Vicenzo—70-71-67-70—278
Nicklaus: 71-69-71-69—280. 2nd.

1968—Carnoustie Golf Links, Carnoustie, Scotland
Winner: Gary Player—74-71-71-73—289
Nicklaus: 76-69-73-73—291. T2nd.

1969—Royal Lytham & St. Annes Golf Club, Lytham St. Annes, England
Winner: Tony Jacklin—68-70-70-72—280
Nicklaus: 75-70-68-72—285. T6th.

1970—The Old Course, St. Andrews, Scotland
Winner: Nicklaus—68-69-73-73—283
(defeated Doug Sanders in playoff 72-73)

1971—Royal Birkdale Golf Club, Southport, England
Winner: Lee Trevino—69-70-69-70—278
Nicklaus: 71-71-72-69—283. T5th.

1972—Honourable Company of Edinburgh Golfers, Muirfield, Scotland
Winner: Lee Trevino—71-70-66-71—278
Nicklaus: 70-72-71-66—279. 2nd.

1973—Royal Troon Golf Club, Troon, Scotland
Winner: Tom Weiskopf—68-67-71-70—276
Nicklaus: 69-70-76-65—280. 4th.

1974—Royal Lytham & St. Annes Golf Club, Lytham St. Annes, England
Winner: Gary Player—69-68-75-70—282
Nicklaus: 74-72-70-71—287. 3rd.

1975—Carnoustie Golf Links, Carnoustie, Scotland
Winner: Tom Watson—71-67-69-72—279
(defeated Jack Newton in playoff 71-72)
Nicklaus: 69-71-68-72—280. T3rd.

1976—Royal Birkdale Golf Club, Southport, England
Winner: Johnny Miller—72-68-73-66—279
Nicklaus: 74-70-72-69—285. T2nd.

1977—Turnberry Golf Links, Turnberry, Scotland
Winner: Tom Watson—68-70-65-65—268
Nicklaus: 68-70-65-66—269. 2nd.

1978—The Old Course, St. Andrews, Scotland
Winner: Nicklaus—71-72-69-69—281

1979—Royal Lytham & St. Annes Golf Club, Lytham St. Annes, England
Winner: Severiano Ballesteros—73-65-75-70—283
Nicklaus: 72-69-73-72—286. T2nd.

1980—Honourable Company of Edinburgh Golfers, Muirfield, Scotland
Winner: Tom Watson—68-70-64-69—271
Nicklaus: 73-67-71-69—280. T4th.

1981—Royal St. George's Golf Club, Sandwich, Kent
Winner: Bill Rogers—72-66-67-71—276
Nicklaus: 83-66-71-70—290. T23rd.

1982—Royal Troon Golf Club, Troon, Scotland
Winner: Tom Watson—69-71-74-70—284
Nicklaus: 77-70-72-69—288. T10th.

1983—Royal Birkdale Golf Club, Southport, England
Winner: Tom Watson—67-68-70-70—275
Nicklaus: 71-72-72-70—285. T29th.

1984—The Old Course, St. Andrews, Scotland
Winner: Severiano Ballesteros—69-68-70-69—276
Nicklaus: 76-72-68-72—288. T31st.

1985—Royal St. George's Golf Club, Sandwich, Kent
Winner: Sandy Lyle—68-71-73-70—282
Nicklaus: 77-75—152. Missed cut.

1986—Turnberry Golf Links, Turnberry, Scotland
Winner: Greg Norman—74-63-74-69—280
Nicklaus: 78-73-76-71—298. T46th.

1987—Honourable Company of Edinburgh Golfers, Muirfield, Scotland
Winner: Nick Faldo—68-69-71-71—279
Nicklaus: 74-71-81-76—302. T72nd.

PGA CHAMPIONSHIP

1962—Aronimink Golf Club, Newtown Square, Pa.
Winner: Gary Player—72-67-69-70—278
Nicklaus: 71-74-69-67—281. T3rd.
1963—Dallas Athletic Club, Dallas, Texas
Winner: Nicklaus—69-73-69-68—279
1964—Columbus Country Club, Columbus, Ohio
Winner: Bobby Nichols—64-71-69-67—271
Nicklaus: 67-73-70-64—274. T2nd.
1965—Laurel Valley Golf Club, Ligonier, Pa.
Winner: Dave Marr—70-69-70-71—280
Nicklaus: 69-70-72-71—282. T2nd.
1966—Firestone Country Club, Akron, Ohio
Winner: Al Geiberger—68-72-68-72—280
Nicklaus: 75-71-75-71—292. T22nd.
1967—Columbine Country Club, Denver, Colo.
Winner: Don January—71-72-70-68—281
(defeated Don Massengale in playoff 69-71)
Nicklaus: 67-75-69-71—282. T3rd.
1968—Pecan Valley Country Club, San Antonio, Texas
Winner: Julius Boros—71-71-70-69—281
Nicklaus: 71-79—150. Missed cut.
1969—NCR Golf Course, Dayton, Ohio
Winner: Raymond Floyd—69-66-67-74—276
Nicklaus: 70-68-74-71—283. T11th.
1970—Southern Hills Country Club, Tulsa, Okla.
Winner: Dave Stockton—70-70-66-73—279
Nicklaus: 68-76-73-66—283. T6th.
1971—*PGA National Golf Club, Palm Beach Gardens, Fla.
Winner: Nicklaus—69-69-70-73—281
1972—Oakland Hills Country Club, Birmingham, Mich.
Winner: Gary Player—71-71-67-72—281
Nicklaus: 72-75-68-72—287. T13th.
1973—Canterbury Golf Club, Cleveland, Ohio
Winner: Nicklaus—72-68-68-69—277
1974—Tanglewood Golf Club, Clemmons, N.C.
Winner: Lee Trevino—73-66-68-69—276
Nicklaus: 69-69-70-69—277. 2nd.
1975—Firestone Country Club, Akron, Ohio
Winner: Nicklaus—70-68-67-71—276
1976—Congressional Country Club, Bethesda, Md.
Winner: Dave Stockton—70-72-69-70—281
Nicklaus: 71-69-69-74—283. T4th.

1977—Pebble Beach Golf Links, Pebble Beach, Calif.
Lanny Wadkins—69-71-72-70—282
(defeated Gene Littler on 3rd hole of sudden-death playoff)
Nicklaus: 69-71-70-73—283. 3rd.
1978—Oakmont Country Club, Oakmont, Pa.
Winner: John Mahaffey—75-67-68-66—276
(defeated Jerry Pate and Tom Watson on 2nd hole of sudden-death playoff)
Nicklaus: 79-74—153. Missed cut.
1979—Oakland Hills Country Club, Birmingham, Mich.
Winner: David Graham—69-68-70-65—272
(defeated Ben Crenshaw on 3rd hole of sudden-death playoff)
Nicklaus: 73-72-78-71—294. T65th.
1980—Oak Hill Country Club, Rochester, N.Y.
Winner: Nicklaus—70-69-66-69—274
1981—Atlanta Athletic Club, Duluth, Ga.
Winner: Larry Nelson—70-66-66-71—273
Nicklaus: 71-68-71-69—279. T4th.
1982—Southern Hills Country Club, Tulsa, Okla.
Winner: Raymond Floyd—63-69-68-72—272
Nicklaus: 74-70-72-67—283. T16th.
1983—Riviera Country Club, Pacific Palisades, Calif.
Winner: Hal Sutton—65-66-72-71—274
Nicklaus: 73-65-71-66—275. 2nd.
1984—Shoal Creek Country Club, Birmingham, Ala.
Winner: Lee Trevino—69-68-67-69—273
Nicklaus: 77-70-71-69—287. T25th.
1985—Cherry Hills Country Club, Denver, Colo.
Winner: Hubert Green—67-69-70-72—278
Nicklaus: 66-75-74-74—289. T32nd.
1986—Inverness Country Club, Toledo, Ohio
Winner: Bob Tway—72-70-64-70—276
Nicklaus: 70-68-72-75—285. T16th.
1987—PGA National Golf Club, Palm Beach Gardens, Fla.
Winner: Larry Nelson—70-72-73-72—287
(defeated Lanny Wadkins on 1st hole of sudden-death playoff)
Nicklaus: 76-73-74-73—296. T24th.

*—Now JDM Country Club